Essential
Brittany

by
LINDSAY HUNT

Lindsay Hunt turned to travel journalism after a career in publishing and a year spent sampling *tapas* in Spain. She has travelled extensively and written about many destinations, including books on Spain, Ireland and the USA.

AA

Produced by AA Publishing

Written by Lindsay Hunt
Peace and Quiet section
by Paul Sterry
Original photography
by Rick Strange and Steve Day

Edited, designed and produced
by AA Publishing.
© The Automobile Association
1997.
Maps © The Automobile
Association 1997.

Distributed in the United Kingdom
by AA Publishing, Norfolk House,
Priestley Road, Basingstoke,
Hampshire, RG24 9NY.

A CIP catalogue record for this
book is available from the British
Library.

ISBN 0 7495 1221 0

Published by AA Publishing, a
trading name of Automobile
Association Developments
Limited, whose registered office is
Norfolk House, Priestley Road,
Basingstoke, Hampshire, RG24
9NY.
Registered number 1878835.

Colour separation: BTB Colour
Reproduction Ltd, Whitchurch,
Hampshire

Printed by: Printers Trento, S.R.L.,
Italy

*Front cover picture: The harbour at
Erquy*

Contents

This book employs a simple rating system to help choose which places to visit:

✓	'top ten'

◆◆◆ do not miss
◆◆ see if you can
◆ worth seeing if you have time

Introduction and Background

Brittany's rugged coastline is its most compelling feature. Headlands, cliffs, bays, rocks, reefs, estuaries and islets frame scores of glorious tide-swept beaches. Tranquil and biddable one day, foaming like a wild beast the next, the capricious Breton seas are endlessly fascinating. For the Celtic tribes who first settled in France's northwestern extremity during the Iron Age, Brittany was *Armor* – The Land by the Sea. Since then, generations of Bretons have earned a seafaring living, from the Gaulish Veneti with their tin-laden sailing ships, through centuries of intrepid fishermen, explorers, corsairs, and naval recruits. Today the waves cast up new sources of revenue in the ferry terminals of Roscoff and St-Malo as thousands of visitors converge on Brittany for the perfect family seaside holiday.

The most charismatic coastline lies along the north coast and on its craggy westerly capes. The two best-known stretches are appealingly designated by the tourist authorities the Emerald Coast (Côte d'Émeraude) and the Pink Granite Coast (Côte de Granit Rose). The first, between Cancale and St-Brieuc, is named after the verdant scenery of its jagged cliffs and promontories, which are deeply indented by sandy bays and river estuaries. It is best seen from the sea, which sometimes takes on an echoing greenish tinge. Further west, between Paimpol and Morlaix, lies the Pink Granite Coast, characterised by the startling rocks that fringe the shoreline. Vivid russet in places, these strange outcrops have been eroded by wind and waves into astonishing organic forms.

Steps lead through old Lannion to the hilltop church of Brélévenez

INTRODUCTION

Finistère's coast is mostly low-lying, its scenic highlights lying mainly at its extremities. Deadly reefs lie half-submerged like slumbering crocodiles, waiting for Atlantic storms, treacherous currents or bewildering sea-fogs to serve up their prey. A chain of lighthouses and hazard markers studs this perilous coastline, but tragedies still occur.

Brittany's southern coast has a more smiling if less dramatic aspect. The milder, less exposed location produces the lushly wooded estuaries around Cornouaille and sheltered sunbathing beaches further east. Near Vannes, a vast tidal lagoon called the Golfe du Morbihan has chewed the low-lying coastline into hundreds of islets – a haven for countless seabirds and migrant waders. North of La Baule, a huge peat-marsh once submerged beneath the sea supports a fascinating ecosystem and way of life – now preserved as a regional park. Here the stately River Loire, once the Duchy's southern boundary, takes a final bow before entering the sea at St-Nazaire.

As a holiday destination, Brittany offers far more than buckets and spades. A rich layer-cake of historical associations stretching back millennia, it makes a fascinating touring base, with enough sightseeing to entice *aficionados* of all ages for repeat visits year after year. British

The Port de Plaisance at the edge of Vannes' old town

LOCATOR

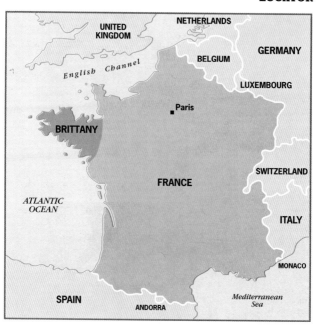

and Irish visitors are among Brittany's keenest devotees. It is not so very different, climatically, geographically and culturally, from the Celtic outposts of the British Isles – yet different enough (and that vital fraction warmer) to sustain interest. Generally, though, it appeals to those who enjoy a fairly active holiday. You can never rely on cloudless sunshine in Brittany, but even if it rains or blows for a while, there is always plenty to do. Dozens of medieval castles, fascinating churches and picturesquely timbered, flower-decked towns await exploration. Finistère's calvaries, soaring steeples and unique parish closes constitute some of Brittany's most fascinating architectural heirlooms. The interior workmanship on carved rood-screens, pulpits and glory beams shows equally magnificent artistry. In bad weather, Brittany has absorbing museums and indoor

Gannets nest in huge numbers on the Île Rouzic (Les Sept Îles)

attractions. On fine days, you can take a picnic for a megalith search, a forest walk or a trip to an island.

Brittany provides amenities for many kinds of sports and leisure pursuits, including over 400 miles (650km) of navigable rivers and canals for boating holidays. For walkers there are footpaths galore, along coastguard tracks (*sentiers des douaniers*), canal towpaths (*chemins de halage*), open countryside (*sentiers de pays*) or woodland trails. Birdwatchers and beachcombers will be in their element. Brittany's varied habitats attract a wide range of birds and plants. Seabirds and wildfowl cluster in great numbers on its rocky cliffs and islands, dunes and wetland areas. Hundreds of species of seaweeds colonise its tidal zones in richly coloured fronds. Hydrangeas flourish almost

like weeds in every garden. Finistère's Parc Naturel Régional d'Armorique, Loire-Atlantique's Parc Naturel Régional de Brière, and the Golfe du Morbihan are particularly good places to find unusual flora and fauna. During the summer season, colourful festivals provide a constant round of pageantry with traditional music, costumes and dancing. These aspects of Breton culture have undergone a great revival in recent years, partly as a result of tourist interest. Many of them have a religious origin, stemming from the medieval *pardon* ceremony in which local patron saints were invoked to intercede for the forgiveness of sins. Others, more recent in concept, are purely secular festivities intended to foster local traditions, and sometimes, to raise money for charitable causes.

BACKGROUND

The Breton peninsula measures about 125 miles (200km) from east to west between the Atlantic Ocean and the English Channel. Its long, rugged shore stretches around 1,860 miles (3,000km) of intricately carved capes, bays and islands, as much coastline as all the rest of France put together. This means that virtually every aspect of it – climatic, cultural, economic – is influenced by the sea. After the last Ice Age, sea levels rose and drowned many of Brittany's low-lying fringes, producing the sunken valleys (*abers*), inland seas and tidal marshes that characterise the coast. Parts of the former mainland turned into islands and reefs. The strong tides that flood Brittany's estuaries make a huge difference to the appearance of the shore, and have even been harnessed for hydro-electric power along the Rance.

The sea produces other profitable harvests too. Besides a huge variety of sea creatures which have fed and supported Breton families for generations, ancillary shore-based livelihoods such as salt production or fish processing still play a part in the local economy. Seaweed cultivation (for fuel and fertiliser, and many modern uses in food technology, cosmetics, and pharmaceuticals) is gaining significance. Shipbuilding and the navy have always been popular Breton careers. Less welcome maritime influences are the oil spillages from wrecked tankers which periodically plague the coast. The most damaging in recent years, the huge oil slick from the tanker *Amoco Cadiz*, wrecked off Finistère in March 1978, killed countless seabirds and threatened Brittany's vital tourist industry.

Despite the all-pervading significance of the sea, the hinterland also plays an important role in modern Brittany. It is one of France's most productive agricultural regions, with over a third of its population actively engaged in farming. Above all, the region specialises in early vegetables. The purposeful roar of containerised juggernauts can now be heard on all its major roads as perishable crops are hurried to ports and markets for distribution and export.

Artichokes flourish in the rich soils of the Ceinture Dorée near Carentec

Geography

Most of Brittany is flattish or gently undulating. The ancient Armorican mountains which once towered higher than the Alps have worn down to a few pudding-basin stumps in the Parc Naturel Régional d'Armorique of central Finistère, where Brittany's wildest inland scenery can be found. For the most part, inland Brittany is a man-made landscape of small hedged or coppiced farmsteads channelled by watercourses – attractively varied but not especially spectacular. The Celts knew this region as *Argoat*, the Land in the Forest, but the huge tracts of primeval woodland that once covered Brittany have now been felled for ships' timbers, or blown down by storms.

In bad weather, Brittany can seem deceptively monochrome – the mournful grey-green of cabbage fields and the slate or granite rocks used everywhere as building materials. Look more closely and you will find an infinitely subtle tapestry. The symmetry of those perfect glaucous crops has its own weird beauty, while the rocks sparkle with crystals of quartz and mica and feldspar beneath a soft patina of multicoloured lichen.

The Monts d'Arrée, Brittany's last inland wilderness

BACKGROUND

Geographically remote, Brittany is also historically distinct from the rest of France. With its own culture and language, it retains a separate identity some would like to see more formally recognised. Until 1532 it was an independent Duchy, and beyond Haute-Bretagne's defensive chain of eastern border fortresses, the differences grow steadily more pronounced towards Basse-Bretagne in the west. Finistère is the region most visitors tend to think of as Brittany – a land of pancakes and *pardons* and parish closes suffused with ancient Celtic legends. It is in Finistère that you are most likely to hear Breton spoken, and see traditional costume worn with the characteristic white *coiffe* or headdress. Whatever the tourist brochures may suggest, however, this is now rare except on special occasions such as festivals or weddings.

Penmarc'h's inhospitable coastline off western Finistère

Standing stones pepper the countryside around St-Just, near Redon

History and Culture

Brittany's historic resonances stretch back many thousands of years. The earliest traces of human settlement date back to about 8000 BC. Stone Age dwellers left evidence of their existence in burial places consisting of gallery or passage graves (also known as dolmens). In addition, they constructed one of the world's most puzzling archaeological enigmas: vast numbers of standing stones or *menhirs* arranged in bizarre *alignements*, or lines, that have never been explained. These megalithic patterns, best seen around Carnac in southern Brittany, are regarded by many authorities as the most significant palaeolithic monument in Europe. Swirling in mists of antiquity, the stones of Carnac deserve at least one look in a lifetime. Later (in about 1800 BC) came Bronze Age settlers who fashioned the smooth, green axe-heads found in any Breton history museum. Hoards of these prized artefacts have been unearthed all over Brittany, where they were once buried like treasure. Beautifully crafted jewellery and decorated pottery also dates from this period, suggesting a highly developed and prosperous civilisation. During the Iron Age, the first wave of Celtic people arrived in Brittany. They settled in five

BACKGROUND

The Last Supper in the parish close at Guimiliau

main tribes, colonising areas roughly corresponding to the five *départements* into which Brittany was subsequently divided. These intrepid seafarers traded local mineral wealth as far as Mediterranean lands. Despite their experience in war, and their hill-forts and earthworks, they were no match for the Romans, and Julius Caesar successfully completed his conquest of Gaul in 56 BC after a decisive sea battle in the Golfe du Morbihan. The Romans left no very great reminders of their presence in Armorica, as they did in other parts of France. But the Pax Romanica, a time of order and plenty, lasted until the 5th century AD, after which chaos reigned for centuries. Barbarians overran Armorica, followed by a more civilised second wave of Celts from British shores, driven out by invading Norse and Anglo-Saxon tribes. These saintly monks brought their religion and their language with them, built many churches,

and called their new home in memory of the land they had left – Brittany, meaning Little Britain.

The Middle Ages were a long round of conflict and confusion in Brittany. The Franks invaded in AD 799 under Charlemagne, to be expelled again within 50 years. Eventually the local warlords welded themselves into a nation and made Brittany an independent Duchy, fortifying it with many castles. During the Hundred Years War with England, Bertrand du Guesclin, born in Dinan in 1320, emerged as a local hero.

Brittany's fortunes gradually recovered under the House of Montfort, trading picked up and architecture flourished in Gothic churches and fortresses. France looked enviously on at its attractively wealthy but worryingly powerful neighbour. Anne de Bretagne (1477–1514), Brittany's last duchess, became one of its best-loved figures as she fought to preserve her people's independence. Her dynastic marriages with French monarchs hastened Brittany's inevitable fate, however, and in 1532 Brittany became part of France.

The 16th century was a time of great prosperity from seaborne trade. The linen trade flourished with the insatiable demand for sailcloth, enriching many communities, particularly the ports of St-Malo, Nantes and Lorient, where elegant mansions and châteaux proliferated. Corsairs (privateers licensed by the Crown) made rich pickings from plundering foreign shipping. The St-Malo explorer Jacques Cartier added Canada to France's colonial possessions. Many of Brittany's greatest churches and parish closes were constructed at this period, along with a host of wayside shrines, calvaries and chapels.

The accession of Louis XIII meant further developments in Brittany. While Cardinal Richelieu set about dismantling its fortifications to discourage local insurrection, the military architect Vauban radically upgraded its coastal defences against foreign invasion. The port of Brest underwent massive transformation as work began on its docks. Brittany's forests dwindled under unprecedented demands for wooden sailing ships.

During the 17th and 18th centuries Brittany quivered with outrage at its exploitation by successive French kings (especially Louis XIV)

BACKGROUND

Flowers decorate the locks and bridges of Redon's canals

and various uprisings occurred. When the Revolution broke out, Brittany rejoiced, only to be swiftly disillusioned by the godless excesses of the Terror. Brittany soon realised that its autonomy was even more threatened by a centralised Parisian Republic than a *laissez-faire* monarchy, and an unsuccessful Royalist counter-Revolutionary movement spearheaded by the Chouans emerged.

Napoleon, conscious of Brittany's proximity to England, his old enemy, began the construction of the Canal de Nantes à Brest to provide safe passage for shipping between the Loire and the Aulne. During the 19th century, further canals and railways improved trade and communications, while literary and artistic movements raised Brittany's cultural profile. Jules Verne and René de Chateaubriand were leading writers of the period, while Gauguin became the most celebrated member of the Pont-Aven School of painters.

Both World Wars devastated Brittany, resulting in a huge loss of life and the total destruction of many of its major ports as Allied bombers attempted to dislodge the occupying Germans. The final struggle was bitter, and has left deep scars. Brittany played a spirited role in the Resistance movement, and some of the most daring escape stories are set on the lonely shores of Côtes d'Armor, where fugitive prisoners-of-war and shot-down pilots assembled in a 'safe house' (the Maison d'Alphonse) before slipping back to England under cover of darkness. When D-Day arrived, Resistance activists in Morbihan successfully diverted many German troops from the beaches of Normandy. Since then, Brittany has steadily recovered, rebuilding both its economy and its bombed cities to play a full part in post-war prosperity.

Brittany Today

Brittany is now France's second most important holiday area, with much new building along its coast. For the most part, construction has been sensitively carried out in traditional local styles. Many of Brittany's lovely old buildings have been successfully restored, showing a truly delightful range of vernacular styles from stone

A new suspension bridge spans the Vilaine at La Roche-Bernard

malouinières (corsair mansions) and slate-hung townhouses to thatched farms or tidal mills. Only the renovated seaports (Brest, Lorient and St-Nazaire) show the true bleakness of the 20th century's architectural imagination.

Besides its major concerns of fishing, agriculture and tourism, Brittany now leads France's telecommunications industry, and has large car manufacturing plants. One important recent development was an administrative reshuffle in 1973, which deducted one of its five *départements*. Loire-Atlantique in the southeast now belongs technically to the neighbouring region of Pays de la Loire. Most of Loire-Atlantique's inhabitants still regard themselves as Breton, but economically, the transition has meant the loss of one of Brittany's largest and most prosperous cities (its former capital, Nantes) and its most sophisticated seaside resort (La Baule-Escoublac). Parisian bureaucracy is a powerful irritant to many Bretons, and a volatile separatist movement is worrying French authorities. The demands of its influential farming and fishing lobbies in the face of unpopular EU regulations are another thorn in the government's side.

What to See

The Essential rating system:

✓	'top ten'

♦♦♦   do not miss
♦♦   see if you can
♦   worth seeing if you
       have time

For most visitors, Brittany means a seaside holiday. With countless beaches in idyllic settings, there is enough coastline to keep an average family thoroughly contented for many repeat visits. It is a pity, however, to ignore the *argoat* (interior) completely. Though some of the scenery consists of unremarkable and intensively managed farmland, there are stretches of much wilder beauty among the hills of the Monts d'Arrée or the lonely limestone gorges north of Mûr-de-Bretagne. Only by venturing inland will you see the best of Brittany's extraordinary parish closes, or the lively cities of Rennes, Quimper and Nantes. Additional pleasures include tranquil inland waterways, mighty castles and a host of delightful rural towns.

While most guidebooks select stretches of coastline for their regional divisions of Brittany, the following section is divided along the administrative boundaries of the five *départements*. As a

result, each chunk of coastline is described with its accompanying hinterland. Each area has a distinctive flavour. Île-et-Vilaine is Haute-Bretagne, which due to its location has always encountered firmly Gallic influences. As you head westwards, however, the Celtic or Breton elements become more pronounced. In Finistère you will find them in their purest form. In the southeastern area of Loire-Atlantique, the Breton influences merge gradually with the Loire Valley, to which this *département* now officially belongs.

ÎLLE-ET-VILAINE

This part of Haute-Bretagne is not the most obvious place for a Breton holiday. Leaving aside the immensely popular entry port of St-Malo, and the stylish resort of Dinard, Ille-et-Vilaine has hardly any of what most visitors like about Brittany, which is its rugged coastline. The brief stretch between the Rance and the Normandy border presents a landscape of brackish salt marshes, obdurately flat. Through it carve

These houses in Rennes survived the Great Fire of 1720

BRITTANY REGIONAL MAP

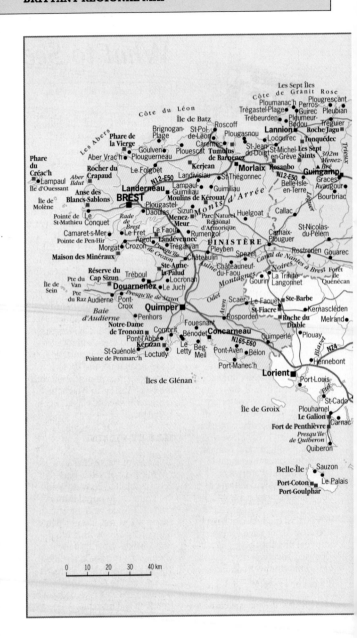

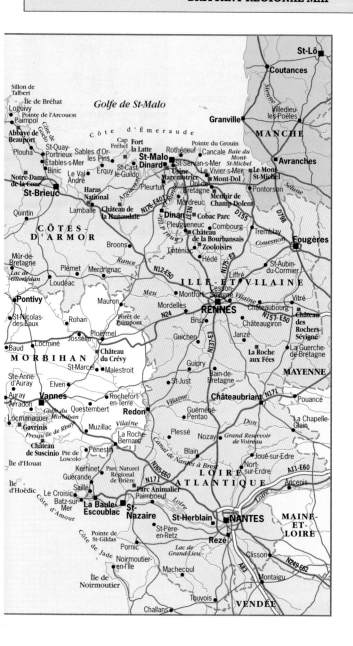

the sluggish waterways which give the *département* its name, linking the Channel with the Atlantic and saving fair-weather sailors the anxiety of negotiating Finistère's treacherous coastline. From the deck of a boat, you can see aspects of Brittany impossible to experience from the roads. For car-tourers, however, these unsung Breton borderlands offer a surprising variety of scenery and sightseeing. No one should miss the grand fortresses that once protected the independent Duchy from its jealous French sister: Fougères, Combourg, Vitré. The Breton capital, inland Rennes, is well worth a day or two's exploration. And once in a lifetime at least, be sure to slip over the border into Normandy for a look at one of France's greatest sights, the island abbey of Mont-St-Michel.

Oysters at Cancale

East of Cancale lie the muddy salt-flats of the Baie dù Mont-St-Michel; to the west the Côte d'Émeraude begins in earnest at the rocky headland of the **Pointe du Grouin** (fine walks and seabirds).

◆◆
CANCALE

Cancale is renowned for its oysters. The grey shoreline is covered with the shallow concrete beds (*parcs*) where they mature. After harvesting and cleaning, they are piled high on local stalls, or more expensively, at the colourful seafood restaurants all along the water-front in the picturesque port of La Houle. The **Musée de l'Huître** (Oyster Museum) in an oyster farm is devoted to the life and times of the local mollusc (*open:* mid-February to mid-November, daily). An elegantly restored *bisquine* (oyster boat) now used for excursions recalls the days when local fishermen trawled the seabed for wild oysters.

> **Oysters**
> The oysters of Cancale are not wild. Earlier this century virtually all the natural oyster stocks in local waters were wiped out by a virus, and now the young seed oysters (known as spat) are brought in from southern Brittany and farmed like any other crop. They are placed in shallow pans to spend several years before reaching maturity – and their inevitable fate on some *assiette de fruits de mer*. Oysters can be eaten either by tipping the shell and swallowing them whole, or by extracting them with a fork. Cancale oysters can be eaten at any time of year.

◆◆
COMBOURG

The massive 11th-century **castle** by the lakeshore, all crenellations and pepper-pot towers, is the main focus of attention in this small inland town. Literary visitors have an additional interest in the building. The castle was the family home of the Romantic writer René de Chateaubriand, who wrote vividly of his miserable childhood in the haunted bedroom. The old town is attractive, though a bottleneck for traffic. Several central hotels promise a decent lunch if you want to break your journey.

◆◆
DINARD

This chic seaside resort was a mere fishing village until the mid-19th century. The sheltered climate and beautiful setting attracted wealthy visitors who built large ornate villas on the wooded cliffs above three sandy beaches. Holiday homes, smart yachts and striped beach-huts

The Pepper-pot towers of Combourg castle pierce the surrounding trees

jostle along the seafront as seasonal visitors, French and foreign, flock to enjoy Dinard's excellent facilities. These include an Olympic-sized swimming pool, a casino and boat trips. Regattas and tennis tournaments are regular features of the social calendar. Two little museums are worth a look: the **Musée de la Mer** (sea creatures and polar explorations), and **Musée du Site Balnéaire** (local history). The main attraction of Dinard, however, is still the magnificent setting peppered with frivolous maritime architecture, best admired from the **Promenade du Clair de Lune**.

Just outside the town, the world's first tidal power dam (**Usine Marémotrice**) harnesses the ebb and flow of the Rance. You can visit free of charge to see the internal workings of this massive engineering project.

The Z-shaped shutters on this old stone mill are typical of the region

◆◆
DOL-DE-BRETAGNE

Dol stands on the remains of a cliff amid low-lying pastureland reclaimed from the sea. It was founded in the 6th century by St Samson, one of Brittany's 'founding saints'. Its gaunt granite **cathedral** still dominates the town. Nearby is a local history museum, and several streets of picturesque old houses. Just north of the town the **Mont-Dol**, a granite mound topped by an ancient chapel, erupts surprisingly from the salt marsh plains and offers extensive views. A legend declares this is the site of St Michael's apocalyptic struggle with Satan.

◆◆
FOUGÈRES

The dominant feature of this little shoemaking town near the Breton borderlands is a magnificent **castle**, built around AD 1000 to protect the Duchy from the encroaching French. Unusually, it lies at the foot of the

◆◆
REDON

This attractive flower-filled town is an important junction where roads, railways, waterways and regional boundaries converge. It makes a good touring base for a day or two, with useful restaurants and hotels. When the River Vilaine was fully navigable, Redon was an inland port. The Canal de Nantes à Brest crosses the Vilaine here, meeting the Oust to the north of the town. Today pleasure craft ply the local waterways, negotiating Redon via a complicated series of locks. The elegant homes of former shipowners line the waterfront and parts of the old town. The **Grande Rue** is one of the most interesting streets. Redon's main landmark is the church of **St-Sauveur**, a curious mixture of styles. A Romanesque lantern tower sits unexpectedly on Gothic buttressing, with a separate belltower nearby. The **Musée de la Batellerie de l'Ouest** on quai Jean-Bart charts the history of the port and its waterborne trade.

◆◆
RENNES

Rennes is the present capital of Brittany, a burgeoning industrial and academic centre with a cosmopolitan air. The population has more than doubled since the end of the last war to over 200,000. Its inland location amid low-lying, humdrum scenery entices comparatively few holiday-makers from the coastal areas; its central sights, however, are well worth a day's excursion (museums close on Tuesday).

hill, set in a tight loop of the River Nançon. Three massive concentric tower-studded walls form an impressive barrier, but it was frequently attacked and seized (*open*: February to December, daily). A charming old quarter of mills and tanneries lies near the castle around the church of **St-Sulpice**, which contains two rare medieval altarpieces. The upper town of mostly 18th-century houses, built on the proceeds of the wool, hemp and leather trades, clambers uphill towards the tall spire of **St-Léonard**.

ÎLLE-ET-VILAINE

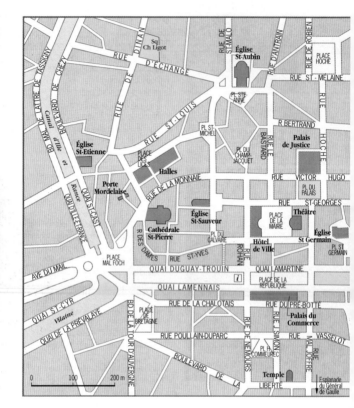

RENNES

Driving and parking in the city centre are not very relaxing, but Rennes is easily accessible by public transport from most Breton cities and major towns. If you want to stay a night, there is plenty to do in the evenings; the old quarter keeps going for longer than most Breton cities or towns, especially in term-time when many students pack the bars and restaurants. During July, Rennes hosts a major arts festival called Les Tombées de la Nuit, where rock and jazz fans congregate. In some ways Rennes's sophisticated urbanity feels more French than Breton, but it remains a keen nerve-centre of nationalist sentiments which periodically wax and wane, fostered by Breton special studies at the university.

The city developed in Roman times from a Gaulish settlement, and then, as now, became a

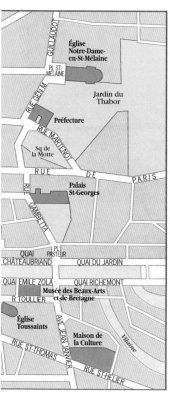

One of Rennes' charming old inns where you can enjoy a drink, a rest and the atmosphere

strategic route-hub. During the Middle Ages, first Vannes, then Nantes, acted as Breton capitals, but Rennes superseded them in 1562, and from then on played a leading role in Brittany's struggles to retain an independent voice after unification with France. In 1720 disaster struck when a drunken carpenter accidentally started a fire in the old town. It burned for nearly a week destroying many beautiful old houses. Eventually quenched by a rainstorm, the charred centre was redesigned in the fashionable 18th-century neo-classical style by Jacques Gabriel. Today, examples of this grand civic architecture stand cheek by jowl with the tall, stripy buildings that survived the fire. The stern **Hôtel de Ville** (town hall) with its imposing clocktower, and the less austere theatre opposite, dominate place de la Mairie, while the huge **Palais du Commerce**

La Roche aux Fées, one of Brittany's largest megalithic monuments

(trade centre) lours along the waterfront. Northwards the eye-catching timber-framed houses of **place du Champ-Jacquet** represent the older style. Another survivor of the great fire is the **Palais de Justice** (law courts), once the Breton Parliament building. Several of its ornate salons can be visited free of charge on a guided tour; the Grand' Chambre and the Salle des Gros Piliers are especially sumptuous. Sadly, the building was damaged in fish-price riots during 1994 and requires restoration.

Cathédrale St-Pierre, Rennes's cathedral, is an undistinguished 19th-century building tucked to the west of the old town in a maze of quaint streets. Inside, a remarkable Flemish altarpiece in a side-chapel is worth finding; switch the light on for the full effect. Close by is the **Porte Mordelaise**, a vestige of the city's 15th-century fortifications. Beyond lies a large open square, the **place des Lices**, where tournaments were held. The elaborate timbered houses around the square were built for members of the Breton Parliament in 1658. The lively art nouveau market buildings are still in use. On the opposite (east) side of the old town, the **Jardin du Thabor** makes a peaceful retreat. These attractive gardens were once part of the grounds of the Benedictine abbey of **St-Mélaine**. One section is landscaped in 'studied carelessness', evoking a natural scene, part is a meticulously organised botanical garden. A spectacular rose garden is its most popular feature.

Central Rennes also has two excellent museums, both housed in the same building along the quai Émile Zola. The **Musée de Bretagne** presents a coherent and entertaining picture of Breton history and culture from prehistoric times onwards, while the **Musée des Beaux-Arts** (Fine Arts) contains a nationally important collection, including works by the Pont-Aven School (see page 60). Both can be visited on a combined ticket (*open*: Wednesday to Monday). Five miles (8km) south of the city is the **Ecomusée du Pays de Rennes**, at Bintinais farm, with a fine display showing the evolution of Breton farming and rural life (*open*: mid-January to December, Wednesday to Monday). On the other side of the city at Cesson-Sévigné (northeast), the **Musée Automobile de Bretagne** has an extensive collection of vintage and veteran vehicles, many in working order (*open*: daily).

◆◆

LA ROCHE AUX FÉES

Stranded far inland 9 miles (15km) west of La Guerche-de-Bretagne, La Roche aux Fées attracts far fewer visitors than Carnac or Locmariaquer. It is, however, a most impressive megalithic monument, consisting of 42 slabs of mauve schist carefully balanced into what looks like an *allée couverte* or gallery grave high enough to walk upright inside (freely accessible). Traditionally, engaged couples come here and separately count the stones. If they agree on the number, a happy future is presaged.

◆◆◆
ST-MALO

For many visitors, whether arriving by ferry from England or Ireland, or approaching via Normandy along the north coast, St-Malo is the first experience of Brittany. In fact it receives more tourists than anywhere else in the region. It is no bad landfall; its attractive setting and architecture, excellent hotels and restaurants, sandy beaches and vivacious atmosphere make it the most attractive of any of the Channel ports.

During the 6th century a Welsh monk, St Maclow, settled in Aleth (St-Servan-sur-Mer) and founded an abbey. His modified name was eventually bestowed on the walled island citadel to which the local inhabitants retreated to escape Norse invaders. As peace returned, the island was connected to the mainland by a causeway, and a strong seafaring tradition developed. St-Malo struck up trading links with Spain and the Americas, and during the 16th century was even an independent republic. Few towns of its size have produced so many notable citizens including explorers, writers and scientists. Another profession for which St-Malo became renowned was privateering. Corsairs licensed by the King of France harassed foreign shipping until the 19th century. During World War II, St-Malo was occupied by the Germans and heavily bombarded in August 1944 by Allied forces, who reduced the beautiful old town to rubble. Painstaking

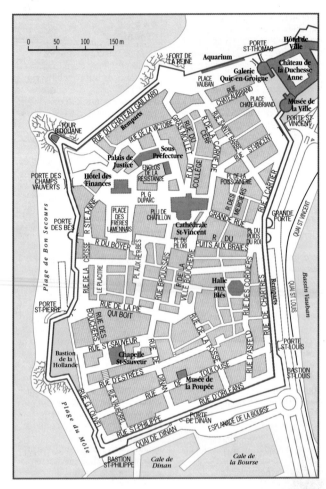

ST. MALO

restoration in the old style provides the almost perfect illusion that you are in a genuinely old town.
For visitors, the main focus of attention is the walled **citadel** on an apron of land behind the port (*'intra muros'*, say the signs, meaning 'within the walls'). It's best to park outside the walls and explore the old town on foot. Enter via one of the gates

St-Servan harbour from the Aleth headland

which pierce the walls on all sides. At some point, preferably when the light is good for photography, climb up to the ramparts and walk around the sentry path.

This gives a splendid overview of the town with its haughty 18th-century buildings in grey stone. The seaward aspect is just as appealing. Below the walls lie the harbour and marina, and several small beaches. Information panels in the walls point out features of interest, and statues of well-known corsairs gaze seawards. To the west stretches the Côte d'Émeraude in all its glory. Threading through the charming old town streets, you will find a small **aquarium**, a **Musée de la Poupée** (doll museum), and the **Cathédrale St-Vincent** which contains bright modern glass and the tomb of the navigator

Jacques Cartier who claimed Canada for France. The **Château de la Duchesse Anne**, near the **Porte St-Vincent**, houses the **Musée de la Ville** (town museum), with a section on St-Malo's seafaring past (*closed*: Tuesday in winter). The adjacent **Quic-en-Groigne** tower has a collection of historical waxworks.

Beyond the walls, small fortified islets lie just offshore, reachable at low tide. One contains the **Fort National** built in 1689 by

Corsair Robert Surcouf spies booty from the ramparts of St-Malo

Les Rochers Sculptés at Rothéneuf

Louis XIV's military architect Vauban. **Grand-Bé** is the last resting place of the Romantic writer René de Chateaubriand. To the west of St-Malo, the **Tour Solidor** guards the harbour of St-Servan-sur-Mer. A former prison, it now contains a museum devoted to the ships that voyaged around Cape Horn (*closed*: Tuesday in winter). A marvellous walk leads around the Aleth headland.

East of St-Malo, the resorts of **Paramé** and **Rothéneuf** merge into the built-up area; each has its own beaches. At Rothéneuf you can visit the **Manoir Limoëlou**, home of Jacques Cartier (*open*: July and August, daily; June and September, Wednesday to Sunday; October to May, Monday to Friday). A local coastal curiosity is **Les Rochers Sculptés**, a weird collection of grotesque figures carved in the natural rock.

VITRÉ

The silhouette of old Vitré makes a striking impact on the skyline. The formidable **château** dates mainly from the 13th century, but was much enlarged and modified during the 16th century and restored after years of neglect in the late 19th century. The castle houses several museum collections, including a startling assembly of natural history specimens (*closed*: Tuesday in winter). The old town stretches through cobbled hilly streets below the castle, its half-timbered houses splaying in all directions. About 4 miles (7km) southeast of Vitré stands Madame de Sévigné's former home, the **Château des Rochers-Sévigné** (*closed*: Tuesday in winter).

PRACTICALITIES

Accommodation

Cancale
Continental, quai Thomas (tel: 02 99 89 60 16). Cheerful, medium-priced terrace hotel amid a line of seafood restaurants.
Pointe du Grouin, Pointe du Grouin (tel: 02 99 89 60 55). Popular with walkers and birdwatchers on headland overlooking Île des Landes. Moderately priced.
Tirel-Guérin, Gare de la Gouesnière, St-Méloir-des-Ondes (tel: 02 99 89 10 46). Modern, mid-priced hotel about 2½ miles (4km) inland. Excellent food. Indoor pool.

Combourg
Du Château, 1 place Chateaubriand (tel: 02 99 73 00 38). Well-established, medium-priced hotel near castle and lakeshore. Comfortably furnished.
Château de la Motte Beaumanoir, Pleugueneuc (tel: 02 99 69 46 01). Opulent château in extensive grounds. Many facilities. Pricey.
Du Lac, 2 place Chateaubriand (tel: 02 99 73 05 65). Simple, with lake views. Good-value restaurant, bedrooms dated.

Dinard
Manoir de la Rance, Pleurtuit, La Jouvente (tel: 02 99 88 53 76). Peaceful converted manor (expensive) overlooking Rance. Garden. No restaurant.
La Plage, 3 boulevard Féart (tel: 02 99 46 14 87). Attractive *Logis* near casino; partial sea views.

Redon
La Belle Anguille, route de Ste-Marie (tel: 02 99 72 31 02). Simple family-run restaurant-with-rooms in idyllic riverside setting 2 miles (3km) outside town.

Rennes
Ar Milin, 30 rue de Paris, Châteaubourg (tel: 02 99 00 30 91). Large, well-equipped but sensibly priced hotel landscaped around riverside.
Pen'Roc, Le Peinière-en-St-Didier (tel: 02 99 00 33 02). Stylish, modern hotel, reasonably priced with ambitious food.
Le Pingouin, 7 place des Lices (tel: 02 99 79 14 81). Modern, civilised hotel with practical fittings. Averagely priced for its prime location.

St-Malo
Ajoncs d'Or, 10 rue des Forgeurs (tel: 02 99 40 85 03). Reliable but expensive hotel in old town. Garage parking. No restaurant.
Brocéliande, 43 chaussée du Sillon, Paramé (tel: 02 99 20 62 62). Small, stylish hotel facing long beach. Set back from road. No restaurant. Mid-price range.
Les Charmettes, 64 boulevard Hébert (tel: 02 99 56 07 31). Inexpensive *pension* overlooking sea near Paramé.
La Rance, 15 quai Sébastopol, St-Servan-sur-Mer (tel: 02 99 81 78 63). Civilised small hotel, moderately priced, near quiet Port Solidor. No restaurant.
Le Valmarin, 7 rue Jean XXIII, St-Servan-sur-Mer (tel: 02 99 81 94 76). Former corsair's home with huge rooms in peaceful

Cobbled streets in a typical corner of Old Vitré

grounds. Elegant ambience and prices to match. No restaurant.
La Villefromoy, 7 boulevard Hébert (tel: 02 99 40 92 20). Located out on the Paramé side of town, tastefully furnished mansion with bright rooms. Garden for drinks and breakfasts. Not cheap.

Tinténiac
Aux Voyageurs (tel: 02 99 68 02 21). Simple, popular village *Logis* with bustling atmosphere. Private garden. Restaurant.

Eating Out

Cancale
Maison de Bricourt, rue Duguesclin (tel: 02 99 89 64 76). Memorable, top-rated food, elegant ambience. Luxury accommodation. Expensive.

Le Narval, 20 quai Gambetta (tel: 02 99 89 63 12). Good seafood at average cost, appetisingly displayed.

Dinard
Altaïr, 18 boulevard Féart (tel: 02 99 46 13 58). Traditional dining room of polished Breton furniture; reasonably priced. Well-equipped accommodation.

Fougères
Les Voyageurs, 9 place Gambetta (tel: 02 99 99 14 17). Good value in upper town. Book ahead. Adjacent hotel rooms rather noisy.

Hédé
La Vieille Auberge, route de St-Malo (tel: 02 99 45 46 25). Pretty terraced restaurant in granite house by pond. Fish specialities are affordable.

Redon
La Bogue, 3 rue des États (tel: 02 99 71 12 95). Enterprising, moderately priced regional cooking in traditional setting. Chestnut specialities in season.
Jean-Marc Chandouineau , 10 avenue de la Gare (tel: 02 99 71 02 04). Accomplished, smart hotel-restaurant near station that will not break the bank.

Rennes
Chouin, 12 rue d'Isly (tel: 02 99 30 87 86). Smart restaurant attached to fish shop. Good value at lunchtime.
Le Corsaire, 52 rue Antrain (tel: 02 99 36 33 69). Accomplished classic food in chic setting for moderate outlay. Good wine list.
La Khalifa, 20 haut de la place des Lices (tel: 02 99 30 87 30).

Interesting, cheap Moroccan food in lively student quarter.

Le Louisiane, 7 place St-Michel (tel: 02 99 79 25 94). Cheap Cajun cooking in old town.

Maison de la Galette, 6 place Ste-Anne (tel: 02 99 79 01 43). Lively, inexpensive old-town crêperie. Prompt service and medieval views.

Ti-Koz, 3 rue St-Guillaume (tel: 02 99 79 33 89). Pretty historic building in old quarter around the cathedral. Not too expensive.

St-Malo

L'Âtré, 7 esplanade St-Menguy, Port Solidor, St-Servan-sur-Mer (tel: 02 99 81 68 39). Appealing, moderately priced seafood restaurant with views over Rance estuary.

Crêperie Chez Chantal, 2 place aux Herbes (tel: 02 99 40 93 97). Grand choice of crêpe fillings, especially seafood, at modest prices. Pleasant two-tier dining room.

A la Duchesse Anne, 5 place Guy La Chambre (tel: 02 99 40 85 33). Smart, popular mid-priced eating place by ramparts. No set menus. Book ahead.

Tea-Time, 4 Grande-Rue (tel: 02 99 40 89 12). French elegance in this English-style tea shop near the walls. Good value English breakfasts and marvellous cakes.

Vitré

Petit-Billot, 5 place Maréchal Leclerc (tel: 02 99 74 68 88). Hotel-restaurant close to old walled town. Good-value set menus.

Taverne de l'Écu, 12 rue Beaudrairie (tel: 02 99 75 11 09). Pretty 17th-century building near castle with average prices.

CÔTES-D'ARMOR

Few visitors would dispute that Côtes-d'Armor's coastline is the most dramatically beautiful in Brittany. With a great variety of inland scenery and several charming old towns (Dinan, Tréguier, Lannion, Paimpol), Côtes-d'Armor is blessed indeed. Not surprisingly, it is one of Brittany's most popular holiday areas. In summer, its main centres and hotels can become crowded. It is never hard to find a secluded beach, however, or a stretch of lonely coast. The less well-known areas make excellent touring and are interesting for their historic associations. The Côte de Goëlo, south of Paimpol, was a centre of Resistance operations during the last war. As you travel westwards through Côtes-d'Armor toward Basse-Bretagne (Lower Brittany), the Breton character becomes steadily more pronounced. Celtic place names appear on signposts, and colourful *pardons* take place.

◆◆
BRÉHAT, ÎLE DE

This miniature island paradise lies about 1¼ miles (2km) north of Paimpol. Ferries shuttle to and fro from Pointe de l'Arcouest, hourly in summer, and there are boat excursions from other nearby resorts. From the mainland it is clearly visible: low-lying and wooded, surrounded by half-submerged reefs of pink granite. The mild, surprisingly dry Gulf Stream climate produces an abundance of flowers, and a great variety of birds visit the

island. Bréhat is criss-crossed by paths, and small enough to walk or cycle across in an hour. Cars are banned. Beaches of pink granite fringe the indented coastline. Bréhat is really two main islands linked by a bridge. The northern island is wilder and less crowded. The southern island is scattered with elegant villas and subtropical gardens, and contains Bréhat's main community, Le Bourg. Apart from a few minor landmarks, there is little to do beyond walking, birdwatching and enjoying the peace and quiet, but there are plenty of visitors in summer, when the resident population of about 300 swells tenfold.

◆◆◆
CÔTE D'ÉMERAUDE ✓

The Emerald Coast lies between the Pointe du Grouin, north of Cancale, and Le Val André – a picturesque stretch of rocky headlands, sandy bays, estuaries, capes and islets. The scenery reaches a climax at Cap Fréhel, where grey cliffs streaked with red porphyry soar to 230 feet (70m), seabirds clustering on every ledge. The top of the lighthouse makes an even more spectacular vantage point. East of Cap Fréhel stands Fort La Latte, a romantic coastal fortress (see page 42). Minor roads run close to most of the

Views from Trégastel on the Côte de Granit Rose

charming traditional village of Erquy specialises in scallops. The description 'Emerald' refers to the lush vegetation on the clifftops rather than the colour of the sea, but often the waves take on a luminous greenish hue. Some of the views along this coast inspired the Impressionist painters.

◆◆◆
CÔTE DE GRANIT ROSE ✓

The rose-coloured rocks between Paimpol and Trébeurden give the Pink Granite Coast its name. Ploumanac'h and Trégastel-Plage are the best places to see this russet rockery at its most striking, especially at sunset when the stones take on a fiery glow. The Sentier des Douaniers (watchpath) leading around the cliffs from Perros-Guirec to the Pointe de Ploumanac'h takes you past a grand jumble of rounded boulders weathered into strange organic-looking shapes. The local rock is widely used as a building material, and when cut and polished, it makes a most elegant finish (popular for Parisian shopfronts and luxury bathrooms). The region around Perros-Guirec is one of Brittany's most popular areas with excellent facilities for family holidays. Eastwards lie the quiet peninsulas of Plougrescant and Pleubian, where tiny lanes meander around sea-capes splashed with gorse and heather. A tourist route called the Circuit de la Côte des Ajoncs makes a pleasant picnic excursion on a fine day.

coast, but some of the best views are from the sea. The larger resorts offer boat excursions. West of the main towns of St-Malo and Dinard lies a long string of small resorts, many named after saints and all with lovely sandy beaches. St-Cast-le-Guildo and Le Val André are the largest and best equipped for holidays. Two of the most beautiful beaches lie at Sables-d'Or-les-Pins and Le Val André. Fishing is a popular activity all along this coast. The Baie de la Frênaye is renowned for mussel-farming, while the

♦♦♦
DINAN ✓

This delightful old town is well worth a lengthy excursion from almost anywhere in northern Brittany. An enjoyable way to reach it, if you have time to spare, is to take a boat excursion to Dinan down the Rance valley from St-Malo or Dinard. Tide tables make it impossible to go both ways by boat in a single day, but you can return by bus or train, and Dinan makes a charming place to spend a night or two. The restaurants of the old quarter are particularly atmospheric in the evenings, and there are several pleasant central hotels.

Standing high above the Rance estuary at what was for many centuries the lowest bridging point, Dinan was a strategic junction even in Roman times. By the 10th century it had an important Benedictine monastery, and by the 12th century it was protected by high ramparts. The warrior knight of the Hundred Years War, Bertrand du Guesclin, was born near the town in 1320. The annual Fête des Remparts, a medieval fair, recreates Dinan's feudal heyday in a colourful pageant.

DINAN

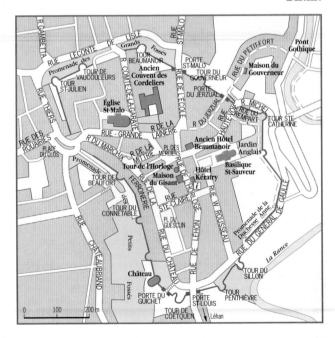

The ramparts offer good views of the old town and the viaduct-spanned Rance valley, and can easily be followed along attractively landscaped paths. The **château** makes a good starting point, with a museum of local history located in the machicolated keep. The 18th-century slated steeple of the Gothic-Romanesque **Basilique St-Sauveur** is one of Dinan's most prominent landmarks. Du Guesclin's heart is buried inside, and some of the carved capitals show strange mythical beasts. Behind the east end is the **Jardin Anglais** (English Garden), a former graveyard. There are splendid views from here. Dinan's other old town church, **Église St-Malo**, is Gothic, best seen from the grounds of the **Ancien Couvent des Cordeliers** (a former Franciscan monastery, now

The port of Dinan seen from the ramparts

used as a school). Many quaint old buildings with sagging timbers and porticoes can be found in the old streets and squares near by. Some are now converted into hotels, shops or restaurants, while the tourist office occupies the **Hôtel Kératry**. Climb the **Tour de l'Horloge** (clock tower) for a good town view. The large, tree-lined main square, **place du Guesclin**, is named after its local hero and contains an equestrian statue of him. It was a Fairground in medieval times, and now the weekly market is held here on Thursday; at other times the square makes a useful parking area.

The steep, winding street leading down to the port, **rue du Jerzual**, leads through one of

An old cider press in the Rance Valley

Dinan's most delightful areas. Beyond a 14th-century gateway it continues as **rue du Petit-Fort**, still lined with picturesque, timbered merchant houses. Terrace restaurants and cafés overlook the Rance from the attractive quaysides. A small tourist 'train' saves the arduous climb back to the old town (summer only).

The ruined priory at **Léhon**, just outside the town, was first founded in the 9th century. A tour of the Rance valley is highly recommendable, for its tranquil estuary scenery and for numerous opportunities to taste locally produced cider.

◆ GUINGAMP

A brief detour from the busy N12 road which carves across northern Brittany takes you to the heart of this well-kept inland town. Guingamp is a sizeable place with diverse industrial and commercial interests. It is also the regional centre and market town of an important agricultural area. During the Middle Ages, Guingamp prospered from textiles; the place name is said to be a corruption of the word 'gingham', which was first produced here. A handful of sights, and some good shops, lie a stone's throw southeast of the **place du Centre**. On the square itself stand a number of attractive half-timbered houses and a fine Renaissance fountain sporting winged griffons and nymphs. The imposing **town hall** is dated 1699, decked with cheerful window boxes in summer and housed in the old hospital (Hôtel-Dieu), a former monastery belonging to the Hospitallers (Knights of St John). Visitors may take a peep inside at the cloisters, grand staircase and Italianate chapel. The great hall contains a collection of Breton art. A few scraps of Guingamp's medieval fortifications can be seen on place du Vally, including the ruined drum-towered **castle** and some small sections of ramparts. The most interesting sight is the 14th-century church of **Notre-Dame-de-Bon-Secours**, an unusual mix of Gothic and Renaissance styles. A chapel adjacent to the main building houses the patron Virgin, a blackened image allegedly brought back from the Crusades. In July a grand *pardon* is held to honour the Virgin, with bonfires and a torch-lit procession. The church itself is full of interest, with elegant interior buttresses and a fine doorway.

A number of excursions may be made from Guingamp, which is a good touring base for the *argoat* or wooded hinterland. Heading (8 miles/13km) west along the N12, **Menez-Bré**, is northern Brittany's highest hill. It is scarcely a mountain, but its isolated 991 feet (302m) altitude provides extensive views to the coast and the Monts d'Arrée. A tiny chapel stands on the summit, dedicated to the Breton saint Hervé. **Graces** and **Belle-Isle-en-Terre** (on the N12), **Bourbriac** and **Avaugour** all have interesting churches.

◆
LAMBALLE
Lamballe presides over an agricultural area, and much of its business is related to its role as market centre for the Penthièvre region. Modern suburbs sprawl in all directions, but the old quarter around the place du Martray is a compact cluster of picturesque timbered houses. The tourist office occupies one of the most striking of these, the **Maison du Bourreau** (Hangman's House). As you examine its useful array of regional information, don't miss the two little museums in the same building. One has a lively display of local arts and crafts, the other displays watercolours, drawings and ceramics by the artist Mathurin

Méheut, born in the town in 1882. Several interesting churches lie a short distance from the main square. Notre-Dame has a fine north door and terrace views of the town. Inside is a splendid rood-screen. St-Jean contains a 17th-century altarpiece; St-Martin is an old priory church with an unusual canopied porch. The most unusual of Lamballe's sights, however, is the **Haras National**, France's second largest stud. An imposing stable-block in extensive grounds northwest of the centre provides handsome quarters for over 400 horses of many breeds. The most notable is the beefy Breton draught horse, once used for ploughing and cart-pulling, but these share their stalls with fine-boned thoroughbreds, saddle horses and Irish Connemaras. The stud can be visited every afternoon (guided tours). Lamballe's social calendar marks several horsy events.

◆
LANNION
This attractive, hilly port straddling the Léguer estuary acts as the administrative centre of the Trégor region. After St-Brieuc, it is Côtes-d'Armor's largest town. A strategic bridging point and route-hub, it can become crowded, especially on market days (Thursday), but if you can find somewhere to park it is a lively and entertaining place and an attractive shopping centre. Long wharves and towpaths fringe the waterfront, and fishing boats give the town a seaside air, though it is some distance inland. The lower town is a

well-preserved assembly of old gabled houses, some timber-framed and decorated with carvings, others slate-hung with overhanging balconies. Two prominent churches catch the eye on either side of the river: Ste-Anne monastery on the west bank, St-Jean-du-Baly in the centre. Lannion's most interesting church, however, requires a pilgrimage. **Brélévenez** church was first built by the Templars in the 12th century, though later reworkings have resulted in a mixture of styles. It crowns the hill to the north of the town and can be reached on foot via a flight of 142 steps from the centre, or less arduously by a circuitous road route. Finding it is well worth the effort, both for the views of Lannion and the Léguer valley, and for the memorable features of the church itself. A stoup just inside the entrance was once used for measuring tithe wheat. The Romanesque apse is a maze of pillars and ornately carved capitals. Below it is a crypt containing an Entombment sculpture. Lannion makes a good excursion base. The Léguer estuary and the wooded valleys inland offer excellent touring. Half a dozen châteaux lie within easy reach, including the stately ruins of **Tonquédec**, and the richly furnished **Rosanbo**. The chapel of **Les Sept Saints** near Le Run is built on top of a dolmen. It is dedicated to the Seven Sleepers of Ephesus, a band of Christians walled up in a cave during the 3rd century for refusing to renounce their faith. They awoke miraculously 200 years later.

As so often in Brittany, however, the coast steals the scene. The glorious Pink Granite Coast is described elsewhere (page 37), but the **Armorique Corniche** bridging the borders of Finistère is equally impressive. Some of the best beaches in Brittany can be found here, notably the stunning 2½-mile (4km) strand at **St-Michel-en-Grève**. The rocky hill behind (**Le Grand Rocher**) provides a good vantage point. Inland, the 17th-century church of **Ploumilliau** contains some interesting carvings, including a spine-chilling portrayal of Ankou, Brittany's Grim Reaper.

LA LATTE, FORT

The romantic setting of this coastal fortress makes it one of the most memorable in Brittany. It stands on a rocky promontory severed from the mainland by chasms which form a natural moat at high tide, granting access only by drawbridge. The present structure dates back mainly to the 14th century, but was extensively renovated by Louis XIV's military architect Vauban. The castle guards the western approach to the Baie de la Frênaye, and affords splendid views of the Emerald Coast from its watchtower. During its expansive career the castle has played many roles: hosting pirates, English spies, White Russians and latterly, film crews within its pink sandstone ramparts. It is privately owned and still inhabited, but visitors are welcome for guided tours in summer (May to September).

Fort La Latte, one of Brittany's most romantic fortresses

♦
MÛR-DE-BRETAGNE

Considering it lies so far from Côtes-d'Armor's scenic coastline, Mûr-de-Bretagne receives a good many visitors and is one of Brittany's most popular inland resorts. The leisure facilities offered by the huge reservoir on its doorstep have much to do with this. The sinuous **Lac de Guerlédan** was formed by a dam built on the River Blavet in the 1920s. This made the Nantes–Brest Canal unnavigable by cargo vessels between here and Carhaix. But the twin boons of tourism and hydro-electric power (not to mention a constant water supply) have been considerable. In summer the lake bristles with sails and waterskiers. The wooded shores of the lake make excellent picnic sites. **Beau-Rivage** is a popular beauty spot. **Le Rond-Point** has a well-equipped leisure centre. To the south is the **Forêt de Quénécan**, one of the last vestiges of *argoat*, the natural forest that once covered most of Brittany. There is little to see in the town itself apart from a chapel at the northern village of **Ste-Suzanne**, immortalised by the painter Corot (1796–1875). Further afield, the countryside is worth exploring. Northwards lies a lonely schist plateau with hidden gorges and calvary villages.

♦♦
PAIMPOL

Paimpol's traditional way of life for centuries was cod-fishing. Its intrepid fishing fleets sailed to the perilous waters of Newfoundland and Iceland from the 16th century to quite recent times. Today's trawlers stay closer inshore and oyster-farming in the Trieux estuary has brought new wealth, but the old town is filled with reminders of the local industry. The **place du Martray** is the focal point of the town. Surrounded by charming old houses, it holds a thriving daily fish and vegetable market. Paimpol's fishing community achieved national fame through Pierre Loti's classic novel *Pêcheur d'Islande* (*An Icelandic Fisherman*, 1886), and Théodore Botrel's popular song *La Paimpolaise*. Today the harbour jostles with pleasure craft, but the nearby **Musée de la Mer** (Maritime Museum), in an attractive modern building, contains many fascinating exhibits of the cod industry. An old fishing schooner, *Le Mad Atao*, moored by the museum provides a vivid demonstration of the lives led on board. Paimpol lacks good sandy beaches so has not become a typical seaside resort like many Breton fishing towns. As an excursion base, however, it has great attractions. The scenic road to the Pointe de l'Arcouest leads to the ferry terminal for the **Île de Bréhat** (see pages 35–6); sidetracking down tiny lanes, you may find a poignant little chapel at **Perros-Hamon** listing the names of lost sailors, or the **Widow's Cross** where the women of Paimpol would gaze seawards awaiting vanished sails. Southwards lies the **Côte de Goëlo**, with the impressive ruins of the 13th-century **Abbaye de Beauport** and the scenic touring route known as the **Circuit de Falaises** (Cliff Tour) past grand brooding headlands (Brittany's highest cliffs) and secluded coves. **Plage Bonaparte**, just north of Plouha,

was the scene of several daring escapes from occupied France during World War II. Inland at **Kermaria-an-Iskuit** stands an intriguing chapel depicting a *danse macabre* fresco.

PERROS-GUIREC

The Pink Granite Coast's largest resort has ideal facilities for family holidays. Two splendid beaches, a casino, congress hall, thalassotherapy centre and modern marina entice many types of visitor, while older visitors settle (sometimes permanently) in its peaceful, spacious suburbs. The town, though pleasant, has no special Breton charm or architectural distinction beyond the church of **St-Jacques**, with its curious spiky belfry and trefoil porch. For good views of the coast, head for the **Pointe du Château** or the **semaphore signal station**. Boat trips to the bird sanctuary at **Les Sept Îles** (see **Peace and Quiet**, page 89) are a favourite excursion. The walk along the watchpath to Ploumanac'h past the most spectacular section of the **Pink Granite Coast** is not to be missed (see page 37).

PLEUMEUR-BODOU

From a distance, a huge white golfball seems to have been abandoned on the heathlands northwest of Lannion. A closer view reveals accompanying satellite dishes and modern, shed-like buildings. The **Musée des Télécommunications**, contains an excellent exhibition on long-distance

Pleasure craft jostle for space at Perros-Guirec marina

message-relay from early semaphore to the latest video-telephones. The highlight of a visit is the Radome show, held within the golfball structure – a high-tech account of satellite communication (in French). Before 1991, when it became a museum, this sci-fi building was the nerve-centre of France's advanced telecommunications research. In 1962 it received the first signals from the American satellite *Telstar*. An admirable wet-weather destination for children and adults alike. The **Planetarium** nearby offers more extraterrestrial experiences, and some entertaining information on modern Brittany.

◆
ST-BRIEUC
The capital of Côtes-d'Armor stands at the head of a large bay on a plateau gashed by deep viaduct-spanned river valleys. Today it is a major city with diverse industrial concerns and an important market. Historically, it was a notable bishopric founded by one of the Seven Saints of Brittany, whose name it bears. The cathedral of **St-Etienne** is its most significant building, a fortress-like church with massive towers. Damaged in the Revolution, it still has many features of interest. The Chapel of the Annunciation contains a wooden altarpiece of 1745 by the Trégor master sculptor Yves Corlay. The old quarter around the cathedral contains a number of pleasant old houses with intricate timbering and decorative carvings. More recent architectural features include the mosaics of Isidore Odorico on building façades in rue de la Corderie. St-Brieuc's well-displayed history museum gives a good picture of regional life. The municipal park called the **Grandes Promenades**

Château de la Roche-Jagu on the Trieux estuary

follows the Gouëdic for 1¼ miles (2km). North of St-Brieuc lies a string of pleasant resorts: **Binic, Etables-sur-Mer** and **St-Quay-Portrieux**. Tourism now outweighs their traditional fishing industries. Inland, the 15th-century chapel of **Notre-Dame-de-la-Cour** has beautiful stained glass.

◆◆
TRÉGUIER

Tréguier stands on a hill above the Jaudy estuary, a sheltered haven for cargo vessels and pleasure craft. Founded in the 6th century by a Welsh monk (St Tugdual), Tréguier later became an independent diocese renowned for its associations with St Yves, patron saint of lawyers, then resident in the town. His tomb, surrounded by votive candles and messages of thanks, lies in the **cathedral**. Tréguier's most impressive building was constructed in pink granite over several centuries in a variety of styles, mostly Gothic. The open-work spire at the west end is typical of the Breton Decorated style, fretted into holes to reduce wind resistance. Inside, the vaulting, stained glass and cloisters are noteworthy. In late May, a *pardon* is held in honour of St Yves, and his reliquary is wheeled along the streets. The old houses and shops around the cathedral square (**place du Martray**) make a charming scene. Near the tourist office at the back of the cathedral is a poignant war memorial by Renaud. Tréguier itself makes a delightful base, but the quiet charms of the nearby coast (**Presqu'île Sauvage**) and the **Trieux estuary** are also worth exploring. **Loguivy** is one of Brittany's prettiest ports. Lenin spent a holiday here in 1902. The **Château de la Roche-Jagu** on the west bank is one of Tréguier's most imposing castles, with a Renaissance interior amid its 15th-century walls.

PRACTICALITIES

Accommodation

Erquy
Le Brigantin, place Hôtel de Ville (tel: 02 96 72 32 14). Traditional stone-built hotel with courtyard restaurant. Attractive modern bedrooms. Small pool. Moderately priced.

Gouarec
Du Blavet (tel: 02 96 24 90 03). Tall, interesting building overlooking Blavet. Period Breton furniture. Good-value accommodation and food.

Guingamp
Relais du Roy, 42 place du Centre (tel: 02 96 43 76 62). Well-run stone hotel on market square; reasonably priced.

Paimpol
Le Repair de Kerroc'h, 29 quai Morand (tel: 02 96 20 50 13). Imposing former corsair's house by harbour, in smart traditional style. Comfortable spacious bedrooms; reasonably priced.

Perros-Guirec
Le Sphinx, chemin de la Messe (tel: 02 96 23 25 42). *Belle époque* stone house perched on clifftops. Light, modern furnishings; fairly pricey.

Sables-d'Or-les-Pins
Le Manoir St-Michel, Le Carquois (tel: 02 96 41 48 87). A 15th-century stone manor house in idyllic setting. Mid-price range. No restaurant.

St-Cast-le-Guildo
Des Dunes, rue Primauguet (tel: 02 96 41 80 31). Modern, comfortable hotel a block from beach. Good food and facilities for a reasonable outlay.

Trébeurden
Ti al-Lannec (tel: 02 96 23 57 26). Luxurious but relaxing hotel with wonderful views. Children welcome. Well worth the price for a real treat.

Tréguier
Kastell Dinec'h, route de Lannion (tel: 02 96 92 49 39). Handsomely converted farmhouse 1¼ miles (2km) from Tréguier's centre. Stylish bedrooms. Relaxing, family-oriented atmosphere. Swimming pool. Good food. Great value

Eating Out

Belle-Isle-en-Terre
Le Relais de l'Argoat (tel: 02 96 43 00 34). Inexpensive *Logis* with good regional menus and honest country cooking.

Bréhat, Île de
Bellevue, Port Clos (tel: 02 96 20 00 05). Small informal hotel-restaurant near landing stage, offering quayside terrace and fresh seafood at affordable prices.

Erquy
L'Escurial, boulevard de la Mer (tel: 02 96 72 31 56). Local scallop (*coquille*) specialities in unassuming, affordable waterfront restaurant.

Fréhel, Cap
La Fauconnière (tel: 02 96 41 54 20). Cliff-edge restaurant in spectacular location, popular with walkers and birdwatchers. Simple, inexpensive fare (omelettes, fresh fish, etc).

Lannion
Le Serpolet, 1 rue Félix le Dantec (tel: 02 96 46 50 23). Attractive stone restaurant in quiet side-street, popular with locals. Excellent fish and desserts.

Mûr-de-Bretagne
Auberge Grand' Maison, 1 rue Léon le Cerf (tel: 02 96 28 51 10). Ambitious modern cooking in smart hotel surroundings. Elaborate dishes, but good-value set menus.

Paimpol
Vieille Tour, 13 rue Église (tel: 02 96 20 83 18). Small stone restaurant praised by Michelin for good-value set meals (à la carte can be pricey).

Perros-Guirec
Les Feux des Iles, 53 boulevard Clemenceau (tel: 02 96 23 22 94). Excellent, affordable food served amid distracting views. Accommodation available.

Ploumanac'h
Rochers (tel: 02 96 91 44 49). Wonderful views of pink granite complement elaborate lobster dishes and Calvados pancakes but expect to pay for it! Advance booking essential.

St-Brieuc
Le Grain de Sel, 19 rue de Maréchal-Foch, St-Brieuc (tel: 02 96 33 19 61). Vegetarian and fish specialities, with local fresh organic produce at unbeatable prices.

St-Cast-le-Guildo
Le Biniou, Pen Guen (tel: 02 96 41 94 53). Attractive fish restaurant above beach. Rustic décor but upmarket ambience and reasonably priced.

Tréguier
Auberge du Trégor (tel: 02 96 92 32 34). Central and very reasonably priced.

Le Val André
La Cotriade, Port de Piégu (tel: 02 96 72 20 26). Small harbourside restaurant with big reputation for excellent, affordable seafood. Book ahead.

Drinks outside at Perros-Guirec

FINISTÈRE

Lichen-blotched figures on the church porch at Guimiliau

Finistère is the most Breton part of Brittany, a land of priests and pagans, pierced steeples and spectacular parish closes, where fervent piety mingles with ancient superstition, customs and Celtic beliefs. Here, more than anywhere else, you are likely to find traditional customs and costumes, and hear the Breton language spoken. Most visitors tend to congregate in the south, where the lush wooded estuaries of the Odet and the Aven create the idyllic watercolours admired by the Pont-Aven School of painters during the last century. Quimper, capital of the ancient kingdom of Cornouaille, has much to offer for a day trip. The north and west coasts, more exposed to the Atlantic, can seem bleak in bad weather, but the dramatic extremities of the

Crozon and Sizun peninsulas make memorable touring, and the islands of Ouessant and Batz have their own quiet charm. Inland, the wild uplands of the Monts d'Arrée and Montagnes Noires present some of Brittany's best natural scenery, while there are remnants of ancient forest at Huelgoat. Agriculturally, as well as culturally, Finistère is a significant part of Brittany. A fertile region called the Ceinture Dorée (Golden Belt) stretches along the north coast. The rich soil, coupled with an equable microclimate, produces a cornucopia of early vegetables. But Brittany's age-old maritime economy still figures large in the bustling fishing ports of Douarnenez, Concarneau and Roscoff.

◆◆
ARRÉE, MONTS D'

Aeons ago, these ancient granite hills once topped 13,000 feet (4,000m). Now much eroded, the rounded stumps still make grand vantage points. The lonelier, less accessible stretches provide important wildlife sanctuaries. Until the last century, wolves roamed wild and dangerously hungry in winter. Today you may encounter deer, otters, and wild boar. Much of the Monts d'Arrée massif forms part of the **Parc Naturel Régional d'Armorique**, a diverse conservation zone encompassing hills and woodland, the tranquil Aulne estuary, the coast of Crozon, and the Ouessant archipelago. Ten well-presented little museums sprinkled throughout the park show various aspects of traditional rural life. **Huelgoat** is the main community of a last vestige of Brittany's *argoat* or inland forest. Devastated by the hurricane of October 1987, there are few venerable trees left, but giant mossy boulders, fern-filled grottoes and a placid lake add interest to local walks. South of the Monts d'Arrée, the black schist of the **Montagnes Noires** (Black Mountains) is overlaid with a soft carpet of lush pasture. The **Canal de Nantes à Brest**, which joins the Aulne for its final stretch to the sea, can be enjoyably explored by boat west of Carhaix-Plouguer. **Châteauneuf-du-Faou** and **Châteaulin** make agreeable mooring points. The small churches at **Spézet** (stained glass!) and **La Trinité-Langonnet** are exceptional.

Bénodet's sheltered beaches attract summer sunbathers

◆◆
BÉNODET

In the Middle Ages, Bénodet handled significant trade in salt, fish and wine. Today its economic mainstay is tourism. Its popularity is based on the attractions of its natural setting at the mouth of the wooded Odet estuary, and a series of excellent beaches. Families converge to take advantage of Bénodet's resort amenities in summer; for more seclusion, take the shuttle ferry to **Ste-Marine** across the river, a charming collection of cottages amid pine trees. Bénodet offers plenty of sports and leisure facilities, particularly sailing in the tidal lagoon at Le Letty, and even a little low-key nightlife. Boat trips in the bay, up the River Odet, or out to the Îles de Glénan, are very enjoyable. The

Phare de la Pyramide (Pyramid Lighthouse) gives good views (191 steps). Out of town, the **Musée de la Musique Mécanique** in Combrit consists of an entertaining collection of working musical instruments.

◆◆
BREST

Brest's strategic location on a magnificent natural harbour (**Rade de Brest**) at the edge of western Europe has been its fortune, and its undoing. The Romans first spotted its potential and built a camp in the 3rd century. The settlement was fortified by the counts of Léon in the 12th century, and occupied by the English for part of the Hundred Years War. Louis XIII chose it as his principal naval base in the 17th century. Brest expanded and prospered during the seafaring centuries that followed, though its harbour was maintained for defensive rather than trade purposes, and it never accrued the wealth of other Breton seaports. During German Occupation, Brest became a U-boat base, plaguing transatlantic convoys and becoming the unwilling target of sustained Allied bombardment towards the end of the war. When Brest fell in 1944, it was utterly devastated. Vast post-war investment has rebuilt, if not entirely revitalised the town in a functional modern style of concrete high-rises. It retains none of its former charm, but is worth a visit for its streamlined docks and roadstead views, and several interesting sights.

A university town, it has plenty of cultural activities and events.

Harbour cruises are highly recommendable.

The **castle** and the neighbouring **cours Dajot** promenade give excellent views of the Rade de Brest. Built between the 12th and 17th centuries, the castle miraculously withstood the bombs of World War II and now houses both the naval headquarters and the **Musée de la Marine** (Maritime Museum). Its eclectic displays include splendid cedar figureheads, a manned torpedo vessel from World War II, and a Vietnamese refugee boat (*closed*: Tuesday). Near the castle is the massive **Pont de Recouvrance**, Europe's largest swing-bridge, and the 15th-century **Tour Tanguy**, containing a museum of Old Brest which gives an enlightening view of how the port once looked (*closed*: Monday, Tuesday and Friday in winter). In the city centre, the **Musée des Beaux-Arts** (Fine Arts Museum) contains a collection of Pont-Aven paintings (*closed*: Tuesday). The church of **St-Louis** is a good example of post-war architecture with bright, jagged windows. Further afield, the **Océanopolis** on the east side of the port is a magnificent crab-shaped aquarium and research centre with exhibits on ocean currents, seaweeds, marine pollution and sea mammals (*closed*: Monday mornings in winter). On the north side of town, the **Conservatoire Botanique National**, dedicated to the preservation of rare and endangered species, will delight plant-lovers.

The clocktower entrance to Concarneau's Ville Close

◆◆
CONCARNEAU

France's third-largest fishing port, it lands huge catches, especially tuna, in the modern, purpose-built premises by the Arrière-Port. If you arrive early enough, you can see the *criée* (fish auction) in full swing. Guided tours are offered during the summer. Concarneau's most charming district is the medieval old town, or **Ville Close**, on a rocky island protected by granite ramparts and a fortified bridge. It played a key role during the Hundred Years War. Vauban strengthened it during the 17th century. Today tourists crowd over the drawbridge to explore quaint old streets and attractive souvenir shops. The Ville Close's best sight is the **Musée de la Pêche**, a well-displayed exhibition on the fishing industry with ancient sardine tins and giant scooping nets. An old trawler moored by the walls reveals the cramped and spartan conditions of life at sea. You can climb the ramparts for good views of the port. Beaches stretch either side of the town, but they are not Brittany's best. Boat trips from Concarneau visit the Îles de Glénan and the Odet estuary. In late August, Concarneau's Fête des Filets Bleus (Blue Nets Festival) attracts many visitors.

◆◆
LE CONQUET
This attractive west-coast port has a large fishing fleet which specialises in crab. Its harbour activities also encompass a ferry service to the islands of Ouessant (Ushant) and Molène. The **Pointe Ste-Barbe** gives a fine view of the coast with many lighthouses and marker buoys warning shipping off Finistère's treacherous rocks. Old stone houses line the hilly streets by the port. The church combines a mix of 16th-century features and modern stained glass. Le Conquet is best admired from the opposite bank of the estuary, where one of Finistère's loveliest beaches, the **Anse des Blancs-Sablons**, can be found. South of the town, an attractive drive leads to the **Pointe de St-Mathieu**, where two lighthouses guard evocative abbey ruins. Below, waves dash menacingly on black rocks. Northwards, the coast road leads past numerous shallow drowned valleys (locally known as *abers*). At high tide the fjord-like inlets mirror their banks in broad, glassy expanses of water; at low tide, offshore reefs erupt from the waterline. **Aber Vrac'h** is one of the main communities along this coast.

Aber Ildut is the official boundary between the English Channel and the Atlantic, marked by the **Rocher du Crapaud** (Toad Rock).

CÔTE DU LÉON
Finistère's north coast is known as the Côte du Léon. Eastwards lie the sparkling beaches and subtropical vegetation of the Armorique Corniche – high spots in any touring itinerary. Further west, with a few exceptions, it is less obviously attractive than other stretches of the Breton coastline. Muddy estuaries, low-lying headlands and a hinterland of cabbage fields comprise much of it. The ancient kingdom of Léon was based on an influential bishopric established by St Paul the Aurelian (St Pol), one of Brittany's Seven Founding Saints. The diocesan seat at **St-Pol-de-Léon** still retains its twin-spired **cathedral** (though not its bishop). The Norman-style structure consists of yellowish limestone, an unusual choice of building material in granite Brittany. The interior is full of fascinating details: intricately carved 16th-century choir stalls, a niche of skulls, and a palm-tree canopy above the altar. The nearby streets contain patrician-looking Renaissance houses. New arrivals to St-Pol may easily mistake the **Kreisker Chapel** for the cathedral. The slender tower, pierced with over 80 daisy-shaped holes, dominates the coastal plains. West of St-Pol, **Brignogan-Plage** is one of the most attractive resorts, its shoreline scooped

into secluded coves sheltered by smooth boulders. The belfry of **Goulven** to the southeast makes another dramatic Finistère landmark. France's tallest lighthouse, the 253-foot (77m) **Phare de l'Île Vierge**, stands on a tiny islet off Plouguerneau.

DOUARNENEZ

Fishing has long associations with this bustling port. In Gallo-Roman times Douarnenez prospered on the production of *garum* (fermented fish paste, used extensively in Roman cooking). Throughout the Middle Ages fishing continued (supplemented by the linen trade), and by the turn of the 20th century Douarnenez had a firm toehold in the lucrative sardine industry, with several canning factories on its workmanlike quaysides. Today, the port still ranks high in France's fishing league. Tourism, however, plays an increasing role in the town's economy, capitalising on the good beaches and sailing facilities of **Tréboul** across the Port-Rhu river. Boat trips around the bay are well advertised, and in summer a ferry service links Douarnenez with **Morgat** on the **Crozon peninsula** (see pages 60–1).

Douarnenez has a grandstand seat on a huge curving bay. Legends say that somewhere in the bay lies the Lost City of Ys, Brittany's Atlantis, drowned by King Gradlon's daughter who was in league with the Devil. It is also linked with the story of Tristan and Isolde. These myths lend an air of mystery to the functional practicality of

Rosmeur Harbour where the fish are landed and auctioned. The pier gives good views. The narrow streets of the older quarters and neighbouring villages (**Le Juch**, **Ploaré** and **Pouldavid**) have many picturesque corners and several churches of minor interest. Douarnenez's most fascinating draw for visitors by far is its splendid **Port-Musée**, an ambitious project consisting of over 250 historic boats moored in Port-Rhu harbour. Restored steam tugs, tuna boats and dredgers float by the quays, along with imaginative reconstructions of maritime buildings (oyster cabins, seaweed-gatherers' huts etc). The **Musée du Bateau** section of this complex is housed in an old canning factory, where dozens of old boats, and boat-building techniques, are displayed.

KERJEAN, CHÂTEAU DE

Half a dozen châteaux and manor houses cluster in the softly wooded hinterland of the Pays du Léon. Some are privately owned, others ruinous or difficult to find. The Château de Kerjean is an exception: well-signed near St-Vougay, welcoming to visitors and full of interest. It is one of the finest Renaissance manors in Brittany. Set in 50 acres (20ha) of sweeping parkland, the château's gabled roofline is glimpsed above high ramparts, beyond a drawbridge and a deep moat. It was built in the late 16th century by Louis Barbier, newly rich on inherited wealth. It suffered much damage during

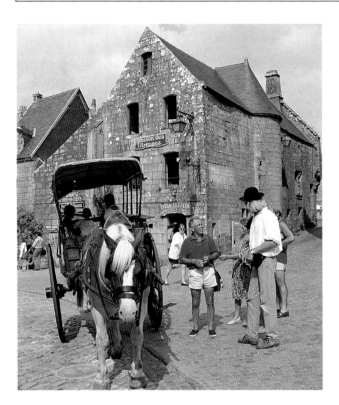

the Revolution, when its last *aristo* was guillotined, and in 1911 it passed into State hands. Since then it has been thoroughly restored and converted into a cultural centre and museum of traditional Breton furniture. An audio-visual presentation fills in local background, and various summer events are held.

◆◆◆
LOCRONAN✓

Even when it is besieged by summer visitors, Locronan's charms are undeniable. Its

A horsedrawn exploration of Locronan's main square

perfect Renaissance square of gold-grey buildings is as pretty as a filmset, which, indeed, it has been from time to time. Many of the former merchants' houses have been converted into smart shops, restaurants and hotels. A browse through its craft studios is an ideal way of choosing some Breton souvenirs. Locronan's wealth originated from the manufacture of sailcloth, and for a glorious period during the 17th century it

single-handedly supplied much of Europe's maritime rigging. When Louis XIV abolished its privileged monopoly, Locronan's economy collapsed. The church of **St-Ronan** is one of the most striking monuments, in 15th-century Ogival Flamboyant style. Stained glass marks scenes of the Passion, while the carved pulpit recounts its patron saint's life. St Ronan was an Irish missionary. His penitential climb each day up the hill behind the town is re-enacted by annual processions called *Troménies*.

A short distance from Locronan, the seaside chapel of **Ste-Anne-la-Palud** is the scene of another pious ritual, one of the finest *pardon* ceremonies in Brittany (late August) with torchlit processions and Breton costumes. The object of veneration is a painted granite statue of St Anne from 1548.

Window-boxes brighten the houses of Morlaix's old town

MORLAIX

The town's location at the head of a dramatic estuary gave it a leading role in the maritime trade of the Renaissance, and from embryonic origins as a Gaulish defence camp it burgeoned into a thriving port prospering on fishing, linen, shipbuilding, tobacco-smuggling and piracy. Like St-Malo, Morlaix was a corsair town, and its daring raids on foreign shipping provoked reprisals. After the English sacked the town in 1522, Morlaix adopted a truculent motto (a pun on its name): 'S'ils te mordent, mords-les!' ('If they bite you, bite them back!'), and constructed the Château du Taureau to guard the bay. Today Morlaix is a delightful place, full of salty atmosphere and compact to explore. The old town lies close to the feet of a giant granite **viaduct** bestriding the estuarial valley. Northwards stretch the wharves of the canalised port, jostling with clanking pleasure craft and cargo boats. Overlooking it is a handsome 18th-century **tobacco factory**, still in use (guided tours). Beyond the viaduct (which you can walk across for excellent town views), quaint steep alleys called *venelles* trickle through a maze of churches and charming timbered buildings, some in a elaborate local style called 'lantern houses'. **La Maison de la Reine Anne** is the best of these (see the skylit interior). The **Musée des Jacobins** (town museum) is well worth a look for its art collection.

The Baie de Morlaix makes a delightful drive, especially at high tide. The western side of the estuary is lined with artichoke fields. The pretty resort of **Carentec** stands on a sheltered headland. On the eastern shore is the **Tumulus de Barnenez**, a megalithic burial complex. The estuary views alone justify the trip. Beyond, the picturesque Armorique Corniche ducks past pretty fishing ports (Le Diben, Térénez), dramatic headlands and exquisite beaches. **St-Jean-du-Doigt** makes an interesting stop; the church allegedly houses part of John the Baptist's finger, a revered relic said to cure eye disease. **Locquirec's** smart villas admire the coastal scenery from their lush, sheltered gardens.

OUESSANT, ÎLE D'

Ouessant is the largest of eight islands scattered off the west coast of Finistère, a treacherous obstacle course for one of the world's busiest shipping lanes. Despite all the lighthouses and warning beacons that guard the reefs, disasters still occur, most recently the *Amoco Cadiz*, which foundered in 1978. The currents here are among the swiftest in Europe and the islands are often shrouded in fog. Ouessant (anglicised as Ushant) is one of Finistère's remotest communities, yet it is easily reached on a fast ferry from Le Conquet or Brest. In fine weather (preferably calm!) a day trip is highly recommendable. Ouessant's traditional matriarchal way of life still persists (women tend the fields and raise stock), although the island now relies increasingly on tourism for its revenue. Ouessant is also an important marine conservation area, and forms part of the Parc Naturel Régional d'Armorique. The maritime climate is surprisingly mild in winter. Seaweed-processing is a local industry.

Ferry passengers alight at the Baie du Stiff where two lighthouses (ancient and modern) guard the eastern headlands. From here the best way to explore the island is by bike (easily hirable at the port or the main village of Lampaul). In a single day, Ouessant is rather too large to see on foot (4½ by 2½ miles/7 by 4km). Simple accommodation and restaurants can be found in

Tall Bigouden coiffes appear at festival time

◆
PONT-L'ABBÉ

The historic capital of Pays Bigouden occupies a strategic location on a sinuous estuary bay where several rivers converge. The monks of Loctudy built the first bridge spanning these complex waterways, and the town was fortified with a sturdy castle in the 14th century. Today this houses the regional tourist office, and the **Musée Bigouden** (*open*: Easter to September, Monday to Saturday), an extensive collection of local costumes and furniture. An annexe museum just outside the town (**Maison du Pays Bigouden**) is a fine example of a typical Bigouden farmstead furnished in local style with utensils and farm implements on display. The extraordinary tall coiffes of the Bigouden region can be seen in the museum. The annual Fête des Brodeuses (July) brings these colourful costumes out of storage. The former chapel of the Carmelite monastery, **Notre-Dame-des-Carmes**, has a fine domed belfry and rose window. Pont-l'Abbé's hinterland is a windswept low-lying peninsula fringed by vast shingle beaches. Once the Penmarc'h peninsula grew wealthy on cod-fishing; today it is largely depopulated apart from a few small ports and scattered hamlets. Sights include the **Manoir de Kérazan**, a furnished château in parkland, a small museum of prehistory at St-Guénolé, and one of Brittany's oldest calvaries, the weather-worn **Notre-Dame de Tronoën** which dates from 1450.

Lampaul. The churchyard contains a monument to the many islanders lost at sea. The main sights on the island are the **Ecomusée de Niou**, housed in two tiny cottages displaying a typical seafaring home of the 19th century, and numerous costumes, tools, etc; and on the west coast, the **Phare du Créac'h**. This contains a lighthouse museum highlighting the elaborate coastal warning system of western Brittany. The remaining pleasures of Ouessant lie mostly out of doors, in its dramatic coastal scenery, wildlife and open heathland where sheep roam freely. Many of the white cottages have blue doors and shutters, the colour of the protecting Virgin's robes.

The calvary at Pleyben, one of Brittany's finest religious sculptures

Parish Closes

Brittany's parish closes represent a unique collection of religious art. The phrase 'parish close' is a translation of the French *enclos paroissial*. There is no precise equivalent outside Brittany. They are mainly, though not exclusively, found in Finistère. Several excellent examples can be seen in the Elorn valley, near Landerneau. Breton closes are walled sanctuaries of hallowed ground around a church. They are used as graveyards, but their main interest lies in their architectural features. These typically consist of a triumphal gateway through which funeral processions pass, an ossuary or charnel house fomerly used for exhumed bones, and (most strikingly) an elaborately sculpted granite calvary depicting biblical scenes.

Secular scenes and local saints are sometimes depicted, and many of the figures are sculpted in contemporary Renaissance dress. Today the granite carvings are weather-worn and blotched with lichen, but still remarkable for their vivid detail and energy. Many parish closes date from the 16th and 17th centuries, when Finistère communities grew rich on sea trade and linen and used their wealth to glorify God with religious art and architecture. Villages rivalled each other for the grandest and most expensive display. Some of the best parish closes include **St-Thégonnec, Guimiliau, Lampaul-Guimiliau, Pleyben, Sizun** and **Plougastel-Daoulas**.

PONT-AVEN

Few of the watermills that once filled the town remain, but its picturesque riverside houses would still be recognisable to the painters who flocked here during the 19th century. The most notable member of the Pont-Aven School was Gauguin, though few of his works are on display at the **Musée de Pont-Aven's** art collection (*open*: February to December, daily). A wander through the old streets and nearby woods, however, will evoke many of the scenes he painted, notably the charming **Chapelle de Trémalo**, where the inspiration for his startling *Christ Jaune* (Yellow Christ) can be seen – a sallow crucifix in the nave. The lopsided eaves of this woodland chapel nearly touch the ground; inside, the roof is propped with

buttresses, the beams studded with decorative bosses and curious beasts. Pont-Aven's popularity with visitors continues unabated, its natural attractions now supplemented by good restaurants, hotels and shops. Downstream, the Aven estuary passes through strikingly beautiful scenery which can be seen best by boat.

◆◆◆
PRESQU'ÎLE DE CROZON (CROZON PENINSULA) ✓

This hammerhead peninsula lunges towards the Atlantic in a froth of wave-lashed fury. It forms the foaming tongue of Finistère's mad-dog profile. As the regional park status

Miniature fortress at Camaret-sur-Mer, erected by the military engineer Vaubon in 1689

suggests, it has some spectacular coastal cliff scenery, particularly at its westerly capes. There is little intensive farming and virtually no heavy industry.

A circular tour makes an exciting day trip, with time for breezy cliff walks and picnics, but the little resorts nestling in the indented coast may tempt you for a longer stay. The pleasant old town of **Le Faou** makes a good starting point, with lovely estuary scenery around Térénez. Detour to the evocative, romantically set ruins of the **Abbaye de Landévennec**, a monastery originally founded in the 5th century. The **cider museum** and **parish close** at Argol, or the **Musée de l'École Rurale** in a converted school at Trégarvan, make other appealing diversions. Continuing along the coastal route takes you past **Le Fret**, with marvellous views of the Rade de Brest, and a ferry service to Brest. The jagged tips of Crozon (Pointe des Espagnols, Pointe de Pen-Hir and Pointe de Dinan) vie with each other for coastal charisma. **Camaret-sur-Mer**, a little lobster port sheltered by a natural shingle bank called the Sillon, has a miniature Vauban fortress, and a clutch of good fish restaurants. The tiny pilgrim chapel of **Notre-Dame-de-Rocamadour** demonstrates the powerful influence of the sea on the local community. In September, a Blessing of the Sea ceremony is held. **Morgat**, another sheltered resort, provides a yachting haven and a good sandy beach backed by pine trees. Boat excursions visit a group of caves with vivid mineral colorations. The placid route along the southern coast reveals several gorgeous sandy beaches.

◆◆
PRESQU'ÎLE DE SIZUN (SIZUN PENINSULA)

This rugged legend-haunted promontory juts like a finger into the Atlantic. Its main focus lies at its extremity, the spectacular coastal scenery of **Pointe du Raz**, where the ocean pounds on jagged rocks. In a gale, it is particularly impressive. Be sure to wear sensible footwear to walk around it as the rocks can be dangerously slippy. A statue of Notre-Dame-des-Naufragés (Our Lady of the Shipwrecked) is aptly placed on this headland. Out to sea, the Île de Sein barely rises above the waves, its reefs and sandbanks a constant hazard. The neighbouring cape, **Pointe du Van**, overlooks the **Baie des Trépassés**, a wild scene of gorse cliffs and heather. Legend says the souls of the drowned rise on this coast on All-Hallows Day. Certainly, their bodies wash up here from time to time. Ornithologists can visit the **Réserve de Goulien** during the nesting season (April to mid July). **Pont-Croix** and **Audierne** are worth brief inspection, the former for its gabled church (**Notre-Dame-du-Roscudon**), the latter for its setting along the Goyen estuary.

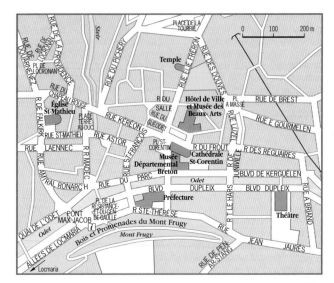

QUIMPER

♦♦♦
QUIMPER✓

Good road and rail links, and an international airport, make Cornouaille's inland capital easily accessible. A shortage of pleasant central hotels limits many visits to a day trip, but this is ample time to enjoy its quintessentially Breton atmosphere, especially on market day. The Breton name for the town derives from the word *kemper*, meaning a meeting place of rivers. The Steir and the Odet make a watery statement throughout the old quarter with pavement cafés and brasseries in Parisian style.

Cobblestone conversations in Quimper

Quimper is a good place to enjoy crêpes and cider (there is even a **Musée de la Crêpe** which has everything from recipes to tastings. On the south bank of the Odet rises Mont Frugy, a wooded hill with panoramic picnic potential. Cross the river into the old town. The twin-spired **Cathédrale St-Corentin** makes an immediate impact, which is easy to explore on foot, dating from the 13th to 15th centuries, though its towers are more recent. Near by the **Musée Départemental Breton** contains an extensive collection of pottery, costumes and furniture. The **Musée des Beaux-Arts** (Fine Arts Museum) is housed in the town hall, with a representative assortment of Pont-Aven School art. The old quarter stretches mainly west of the cathedral, past many quaint flower-decked, dormered houses and *hôtels particuliers* (mansions) such as the ornately decorated **Maison des Cariatides** in rue Guéodet (now a popular crêperie, see page 65).

Quimper dates from Roman times, when a dockland settlement called Aquilonia grew up on the site of present-day **Locmaria**, where Quimper's celebrated faïence industry developed, producing distinctive hand-painted *paysan* designs of blue and yellow flowers, birds, or costumed figures. Oldest of its factories is the **Faïenceries HB-Henriot** (tours March to October). The **Musée de Faïence** has an excellent chronological display of Quimper ware.

ROSCOFF

St-Malo is generally regarded as France's most attractive Channel port, but Roscoff runs it a close second. The pretty old fishing quarter remains intact despite the demands of modern shipping. The picturesquely bereted 'Onion Johnnies' who once loaded their wares on to bicycles for the ferry crossing have long since been replaced by refrigerated containers. Roscoff is a thriving place, successfully combining the role of ferry port with that of seaside resort and export centre for vegetables and seafood. Thalassotherapy and seaweed research are other Roscoff sidelines. The fish-farming enterprises (*viviers*) near the Chapelle Ste-Barbe make an interesting visit. These are the world's largest open-sea breeding grounds, specialising in lobster, crayfish and crab. Nearby on the Pointe de Bloscon, subtropical gardens flourish in the mild climate. In the old town, the main monument is the **Église Notre-Dame-de-Kroaz-Batz**, with one of Brittany's finest lantern belltowers. Galleons and cannon carved on its outer walls indicate its corsair patronage. Nearby stand some of their palatial mansions. One commemorates a visit in 1548 by Mary Stuart, the Scottish princess betrothed to François II. The **Charles Pérez Aquarium** contains a collection of local species.

From Roscoff a 15-minute boat trip takes you to the **Île de Batz**, a simple island of sandy beaches and seaweed processing.

PRACTICALITIES

Accommodation

Bénodet
Le Minaret, Corniche de l'Estuaire (tel: 02 98 57 03 13). Curious and interesting Moorish architecture. Splendid sea views. Lovely gardens. Moderately priced.

Brignogan-Plage
Castel Regis, plage du Garo (tel: 02 98 83 40 22). Superbly located, with spacious, peaceful rooms. Swimming pool, tennis, mini-golf. Fairly expensive.

Carantee
Pors-Pol, 7 rue Surcouf (tel: 02 98 67 00 52). Appealing family hotel in large gardens. Very good value.

Concarneau
Le Galion, 15 rue St-Guénolé, Ville Close (tel: 02 98 97 30 16). Tasteful, sophisticated, and medium-priced small hotel in the old town. Acclaimed restaurant.

Douarnenez
Ty Mad, Plage St-Jean (tel: 02 98 74 00 53). Tall, shuttered, well-kept, mid-price hotel at top of town. Garden, church and sea views.

Locronan
Manoir de Moëllien, Plonévez-Porzay (tel: 02 98 92 50 40). Lovely 17th-century manor in peaceful location. Good value. Excellent breakfast.

Montagnes Noires
Le Relais de Cornouaille, 9 rue Paul Sérusier, Châteauneuf-du-Faou (tel: 02 98 81 75 36).

Down-to-earth, inexpensive central hotel-restaurant adorned with window-boxes. Good lunch or touring base.

Morgat
Julia, 43 rue du Tréflez (tel: 02 98 27 05 89). Good-value traditional hotel-restaurant with sea views. Attractive modern furnishings.

Ouessant, Île d'
Duchesse Anne, Lampaul (tel: 02 98 48 80 25). On quiet breezy hill above Lampaul. Simple, traditional décor and popular dining room. Low rates.

Pont-Aven
Ajoncs d'Or, place Hôtel de Ville (tel: 02 98 06 02 06). Central friendly hotel offering good value.

Quimper
Gradlon, 30 rue de Brest (tel: 02 98 95 04 39). Solid, comfortably furnished town hotel near cathedral. Garden in summer, log fires in winter. Moderate rates.

Raguenez-Plage
Le Men-Du (tel: 02 98 06 84 22). Isolated building overlooking beach. Friendly and inexpensive. No restaurant.

Roscoff
Du Centre, 5 rue Gambetta (tel: 02 98 61 24 25). Popular bar-restaurant near old harbour with simple rooms. Photos of old Roscoff and 'Onion Johnnies'. Low rates. Popular with ferry travellers.
Le Brittany, boulevarde Ste-Barbe (tel: 02 98 69 70 78). Tastefully furnished 17th-century manor house near ferry terminal. Swimming pool. Good food. Moderately priced.

Ste-Anne-la-Palud
La Plage (tel: 02 98 92 50 12).
Luxurious, expensive beach
hotel in peaceful surroundings.
Excellent food.

Eating Out

Restaurants
Bénodet
La Ferme du Letty, Le Letty
Izella (tel: 02 98 57 01 27). Stone
farmhouse by lagoon. Excellent,
quietly sophisticated food at
moderate prices.

Camaret-sur-Mer
Hôtel de France, quai G
Toudouze (tel: 02 98 27 93 06).
Local, affordable seafood in
port. Good views from first-floor
windows.

Concarneau
Chez Armande, 15 bis avenue
Dr Nicolas (tel: 02 98 97 00 76).
Old-fashioned family-run place
serving unpretentious fish
dishes at agreeable prices.

Crozon, Presqu'île de
La Mer, Le Fret (tel: 02 98 27
61 90). Excellent views from
terraces and picture windows
in this modest restaurant.

Douarnenez
Le Pourquoi Pas?, Le Port-
Musée (tel: 02 98 92 76 13).
A suitably nautical restaurant
beside the boat museum
producing brilliantly fresh but
averagely priced seafood.

Le Faou
Le Relais de la Place (tel: 02 98
81 91 19). Plain exterior, but
honest good-value cooking.

Locronan
Au Fer à Cheval (tel: 02 98 91
70 74). Popular, affordable town

centre restaurant with excellent
views of fine main square. Noisy
bar downstairs.

Morlaix
La Marée Bleue, 3 rampe St-
Mélaine (tel: 02 98 63 24 21).
Boasts traditional cooking,
good-value set menus and
interesting wines in picturesque
old town setting.

Pont-l'Abbé
De Bretagne, 24 place de la
République (tel: 02 98 87 17 22).
Excellent fish specialities at
reasonable prices. Good
accommodation available.

Pont-Aven
Auberge La Taupinière, route
de Concarneau (tel: 02 98 06 03
12). Acclaimed regional cooking.
Elegant dining room and good
service matched by prices.

Quimper
Le Capucin Gourmand, 29 rue
Réguaires (tel: 02 98 95 43 12).
Serious, elaborate fish dishes
matched by prices.
La Maison des Cariatides, 4 rue
Guéodet (tel: 02 98 95 15 14).
Well-frequented crêperie, with
curious architecture and huge
range of inexpensive pancakes.

Roscoff
Le Temps de Vivre, place de
l'Église (tel: 02 98 61 27 28).
Possibly the best food in town
and not too expensive, with
excellent views of Ile de Batz.
Seafood and local vegetables.

St-Thégonnec
Auberge St-Thégonnec, place
de la Mairie (tel: 02 98 79 61 18).
Accomplished regional Breton
menus at reasonable prices.
Well-equipped accommodation
available.

MORBIHAN

The name Morbihan means 'Little Sea' in Breton, a reference to the huge tidal lagoon that bites into its coastline. The Golfe du Morbihan forms an intricate maze of muddy creeks and grass-topped islands, a great wildlife reserve. In summer the gulf is a mass of excursion and pleasure boats. One of the most popular trips visits the island of Gavrinis, site of Brittany's most ornate prehistoric tomb. Not that Morbihan has any shortage of megaliths; Carnac's collection of *alignements* (mysterious lines of standing stones) is world-famous among archaeologists. Morbihan attracts many visitors during summer. Its low-lying coastline lacks the drama of the Pink Granite or Emerald Coasts, but is fringed by sheltered sandy beaches and oyster-bed inlets. Trips to its islands, especially Belle-Île, make popular excursions. Its largest city, Lorient, was badly damaged during World War II and although it is not without interest, smaller historic towns offer more charm and sightseeing, notably Vannes, Port-Louis, Josselin, Auray and Pontivy. Morbihan has several excellent museums and numerous notable castles and churches. Inland, it stretches through gentle landscapes of heath, forest and hedged farmland, carved by river valleys and bounded to the north by the most appealing stretches of the Nantes–Brest Canal, ideal for exploring by boat.

Ste-Anne-d'Auray's patron saint attracts many pilgrims

◆◆
AURAY

In addition to the intrinsic charm of its estuary setting and old town, Auray is interesting for its historic and religious associations, and has been denoted one of Brittany's nine *villes d'art et d'histoire* by the tourist authorities. It is now a busy and sizeable town; its principal activities include tourism and oyster-raising. Auray is believed to be the last place Julius Caesar reached in his conquest of Gaul. The Romans established their camp in the river port now known as St-Goustan, which is the most picturesque part of the town. Flower-decked, timbered houses and inns surround the quayside place St-Sauveur and the hilly streets nearby. Benjamin Franklin, forced ashore by a storm, spent a night here in 1776 while drumming up French support in the American War of Independence. Across the quaint medieval stone bridge, the church of **St-Gildas** in the town centre reveals a fine Renaissance porch and a marble altarpiece of 1664. On the northwestern outskirts, shrines and chapels commemorate the martyred members of the Chouan movement led by Georges Cadoudal, who staged a Royalist uprising against Revolutionary forces in 1795. To the northeast, **Ste-Anne-d'Auray** is one of Brittany's most important religious sites. A colourful *pardon* on 25 July (the Feast of St Anne) attracts thousands of pilgrims to its gloomy basilica built in honour of a 17th-century ploughman's miraculous vision. Of more general interest is the vast **war memorial** alongside, dedicated to the 250,000 Bretons who perished in the Great War. Walls inscribed with all their names stretch over 650 feet (200m) around an imposing monument.

◆◆
BELLE-ÎLE

Brittany's largest island lies 8½ miles (14km) offshore, and is reached by ferry from the port of Quiberon, an immensely popular excursion. Attractive beaches and varied scenery, historic sights and good holiday facilities are the main reasons to venture here. Most people go just for a day trip and explore the island on a guided coach tour, but Belle-Île's appealing hotels make longer stays possible

(book well ahead). Ferry passengers land at **Le Palais**, Belle-Île's pleasant capital. Above the harbour looms the star-shaped **Citadelle Vauban**, built during the 16th century. A former prison and garrison, it now houses a museum of local history. The island is divided into four parishes named after the main villages. The interior consists of a fertile plateau cut into sheltered valleys which protect the white houses from the prevailing wind. The east coast has good safe beaches with watersports facilities. The west coast is ruggedly beautiful but dangerous, with photogenically gnawed rock stacks at **Port-Coton**, and a fjord-like inlet at **Port-Goulphar**. **Sauzon**, on the northeast side, is a charming little fishing port with a lighthouse.

◆◆◆
CARNAC ✓

It is not the town, a pleasant if unexceptional seaside resort, but the amazing complex of megaliths on its northern outskirts that attracts most interest. Before seeing them, visit Carnac's well-organised **Musée de Préhistoire** for some archaeological background (*closed*: Tuesday in winter). Also in the town centre is the pretty 17th-century church of **St-Cornély**, patron saint of horned animals, whose life-story is depicted on the wooden ceiling. Carnac-Plage, some distance south, makes the most of a long, gentle beach with hotels, a yacht club and a thalassotherapy centre. Brackish

The mysterious menhirs at Carnac

inlets and lagoons near by make good oyster beds, and less appealing mosquito nurseries. Carnac's megaliths are of two main types. Most startling and numerous are the *menhirs*, or standing stones, whose purpose is still a mystery. Menhirs exist all over Brittany, but in Carnac they are organised in curious lines and patterns, presumably for some obscure ritual or perhaps a measuring device. Three large groups can be seen from the neighbouring roadside (access to the stones is now restricted for conservation reasons). Raised platforms called **Archéoscopes** give good overviews, and provide audio-visual information. The other group of monuments in Brittany are burial sites of various types, including *dolmens* (roofed table-line structures), *allées couvertes* (gallery or passage graves, with longer roofed formations), and *tumuli* (burial mounds or cairns). Examples of all these can be seen near Carnac.

◆◆
LE FAOUËT

Several sights can be seen near this agreeable little market town. In the main square stands a splendid **market hall** dating from the 16th century, a forest of timbers and granite pillars beneath a slate roof. Le Faouët is an artistic town, and fostered a minor school of painting during the early 20th century, encapsulated in the small **Musée des Peintures de l'École du Faouët** in the Ursuline convent. An unrelated, but worthwhile attraction is **L'Abeille Vivant**, an exhibition of working honey bees and apiary products, informative and well-displayed. Several unusual chapels lie within easy driving distance. **Ste-Barbe**, a Gothic chapel in a remarkable setting, squeezes into a rocky crevice in a wooded hillside. Toll the bell by the custodian's house for attention (and the blessing of

Energetic figures enliven St-Fiacre's colourful rood-screen

Ste-Barbe who will protect you from lightning and sudden death). **St-Fiacre**, to the southeast, contains among many treasures a magnificent rood-screen carved with lively, colourful figures of angels and the Seven Deadly Sins. The **Roche du Diable** (Devil's Rock) is a popular clifftop beauty spot overlooking the surging waters of the Ellé.

◆◆
GOLFE DU MORBIHAN

The 'Little Sea' which forms such a prominent feature of the Morbihan coastline resulted from a fall in land levels several thousand years ago. It measures over 12½ miles (20km) wide and 9½ miles (15km) from north to south, a huge, almost landlocked lagoon. Vast numbers of seabirds and wildfowl take advantage of its varied habitats: dunes, mudflats, oyster beds, salt marshes, islands, creeks, reed-beds, heath and pinewood. There are no very good beaches on the muddy Gulf itself, and

swimming can be dangerous; tides tear in and out of the narrow straits near Locmariaquer with great force. Nonetheless, it is a popular holiday area, with hotels, restaurants and campsites sprinkled around the shoreline. The main activity is boating; in summer the Gulf is a mass of pleasure craft weaving among over 300 grassy islets. Of the few that are accessible, the best are the **Île aux Moines**, the **Île d'Arz**, and most interesting of all, the **Île de Gavrinis**, site of an elaborately carved burial chamber beneath a stone cairn. The long **Presqu'île de Rhuys** (Rhuys peninsula) which encloses the Gulf on the southern side has an exceptionally mild climate where camellias, figs and even vines flourish. The **Château de Suscinio** is the main sight, a lonely marshland fortress, now restored as a museum.

◆
HENNEBONT

This feudal fortified town has a long pedigree, but its historic ironworks and location near Lorient made it a target in World War II and little of the old centre survived. The restored pepper-pot towers of the 14th-century **Porte Broërec** can still be seen, however, along with the huge belltower of **Notre-Dame-de-Paradis**. The main sight in town is the stud-farm or *haras* (guided tours). At Inzinzac-Lochrist on the banks of the Blavet, the **Musée Forges d'Hennebont** charts Hennebont's former significance as an iron-smelting town.

JOSSELIN

The most memorable feature of this charming medieval town is its mighty fortress, mirrored in the clear waters of the Oust. Josselin dates from about AD 1000, when a local nobleman settled here, naming it after his son. The present turreted **château** dates mainly from the 14th century, when the town passed into the hands of the Rohan family, who still own the castle. The delicate Renaissance façade which can be seen from the courtyard was added around the turn of the 16th century. Guided tours of the furnished château reveal many fascinating features; in the stable-block is the **Musée des Poupées** (doll museum) with hundreds of exhibits, some several centuries old. The most notable building in the quaint old centre is the church of **Notre-Dame-du-Roncier** (Our Lady of the Brambles), dating from the 12th century and containing the tomb of Josselin's erstwhile master, Olivier de Clisson, Constable of France. A Whitsuntide *pardon* reveres the patron Virgin. Northeast of Josselin on the borders of Île-et-Vilaine, the **Forêt de Paimpont** is haunted by Arthurian legends and a host of minor sights make focal points for pleasant walks and tours. Southeast, just off the N166, the **Château du Crévy** has a splendid costume museum (guided tours). **Ploërmel**, en route, was the site of a famous chivalric tournament in 1351, known as the Battle of the Thirty.

Josselin's mighty fortress dominates the banks of the Oust

LOCMARIAQUER

This pretty oyster port guarding the neck of the Golfe du Morbihan rivals Carnac in archaeological importance. Its main sights lie in a fenced compound north of the village. They include a huge *menhir* on its side, broken in four sections. If it ever stood upright it would have measured over 65 feet (20m) high. Nearby is a large decorated *dolmen* called the **Table des Marchands**, one of several good examples to be seen in the area. Locmariaquer is a peaceful place with attractive south-facing beaches, a pleasant old harbour quarter and plenty of boat trips. Seafront walks and views from the Pointe de Kerpenhir are excellent.

LORIENT

After World War II, this major port lay in ruins – all, that is, except the German U-boat pens which were the target of the Allied bombing raids. Today, these are used by French submarines. Only French nationals are permitted to visit the Arsenal and submarine base, but the rest of Lorient's revitalised dockland and

*A quaint woodcarving decorating
an old building in Malestroit*

state-of-the-art *criée* (fish market)
makes an interesting spectacle
on its vast harbour. The **Maison
de la Mer** in the tourist office
building is an informative if
somewhat over-technical multi-
media exhibition about the port.
A few attractive art nouveau and
art deco houses survive in the
market district. Boat trips to the
Île de Groix are a popular
excursion from Lorient.

◆◆
MALESTROIT
Malestroit's tourist soubriquet
'Pearl of the West' indicates
something of its attractiveness.
Its old quarter is exceptionally
well preserved with gabled
merchant houses of stone and
timber. Many around the **place
du Bouffay** have decorative
carvings of grotesque or
comical figures. In one, a man in
a nightshirt beats his wife. A
hare plays the bagpipes in
another. The church of **St-Gilles**
is also worth a look. It was

originally built in the 12th
century, and modified after a
fire in the 16th century. At St-
Marcel to the west, the **Musée
de la Résistance Breton** charts
the activities of the local *Maquis*
(French Resistance) who
successfully diverted German
troops from the Allied landings
in Normandy. Local monuments
reveal bitter memories of
German Occupation.

◆
PONTIVY
Pontivy's **château** (now a cultural
centre) was a former Rohan
stronghold, like Josselin. It is a
fine example of late medieval
military architecture, with
pepper-pot bastions guarding a
deep dry moat. The corbelled,
timbered houses of the old
quarter near the castle contrast
strongly with the newer district
to the west, which was
constructed during Napoleon's
time in the then fashionable
neo-classical style of wide
boulevards and grand civic
gestures. Pontivy's Republican
sentiments were approved by
the self-styled Emperor, who
earmarked the town as a useful
base in his ambitious scheme to
link Nantes and Brest by canal,
thus protecting shipping from
coastal marauders. At one
period the town was called
Napoleonville in Bonaparte's
honour. The villages around
Pontivy make pleasant touring.
Near **St-Nicolas-des-Eaux**, the
Blavet executes a dramatic twist,
best seen from the belvedere at
the **Site de Casténnac**. **Melrand**
has unearthed an interesting
Ferme Archéologique, an early
farm system dating from about

AD1000. Some way west,
Kernascléden's remarkable
15th-century **church frescoes**
are worth a detour. Visions of
hell in the south transept contrast
with an angelic orchestra and
scenes from the Virgin's life.

PORT-LOUIS

Lorient's opposite number at the
mouth of the Blavet is much
smaller, but much more
attractive than its big industrial
neighbour. It was named after
Louis XIV, the Sun King, under
whose reign the town flourished.
The fortified **citadel** at the
harbour entrance was founded
in 1591, and later used as a
prison, barracks and arsenal.
Port-Louis was the first
headquarters of the Compagnie
des Indes (East India Company)
set up by Cardinal Richelieu.
The venture failed and in 1666
the operation was transferred
across the water to Lorient. After
this, Port-Louis tried its hand as a
fishing port, and having avoided
the devastating air-raids of
World War II, retains much of its
older character. The citadel now
houses the **Musée du Port-
Louis**, a complex of several
interesting museums, including
one dedicated to the East India
Company. Rampart walks give
excellent views of the
roadsteads. Below the walls lies
an attractive sandy beach with a
casino. East of Port-Louis, the
Etel estuary is an intricate maze
of sandbanks, islands and oyster
beds. Too dangerous for
shipping, it offers plenty of quiet
picnic spots, and a delightful
island village called **St-Cado**
with a Romanesque chapel.

PRESQU'ÎLE DE QUIBERON
(QUIBERON PENINSULA)

A narrow neck of tidal sediment
links this feather-shaped
peninsula with the mainland, in
places barely wider than the
access road which runs past
windswept conifers and dunes
of blown sand. The resort of
Quiberon at the far end of the
peninsula is one of Morbihan's
liveliest and most popular.
Besides good sandy beaches
and a thalassotherapy centre, it
is the ferry terminal for Belle-Île
and always crowded in summer.
Other attractions of Quiberon
include boating in the calm bay
on the east side of the peninsula,
where there is a sailing school.
The east coast is called the **Côte
Sauvage**, where the Atlantic
beats furiously on cliffs, crags
and caves. It is very dangerous
for swimming, but a pleasure to
admire from the shore. The
Pointe de Percho offers some of
the best views. The **Fort de
Penthièvre** guards the neck of
the peninsula, and at Plouharnel,
near the mainland, several
commercialised ventures attract
many visitors, particularly **Le
Galion**, a mock galleon filled
with shell pictures. The **Musée
de Chouannerie** recounts the
history of the Chouans, whose
abortive uprising on Quiberon
was foiled in 1795.

LA ROCHE-BERNARD

Since the building of the Arzal
dam, the Vilaine is no longer
tidal, and pleasure craft are the
only boats to reach the town. In
former centuries, however, La
Roche-Bernard was a great

MORBIHAN

riverine trading centre, regularly
visited by cargoes of grain,
wine, salt and timber. The
Musée de la Vilaine Maritime,
housed in the Château des
Basses-Fosses on the west bank
of the river, recounts these
prosperous times. Today, La
Roche-Bernard's revenue comes
mainly from tourism, and it
makes a most attractive touring
base, with an excellent range of
restaurants and hotels. The old
quarter is packed with
charming, flower-decked
houses. A graceful suspension
bridge spans the river, replacing
an earlier version accidentally
destroyed when lightning struck
a German ammunition base.

◆◆
ROCHEFORT-EN-TERRE
The setting on a spur amid
plunging wooded slopes and
rushing water enhances the
postcard scene. Patrician
mansions decorated with
carvings and window boxes line
a cobbled street restored to
tastefully pristine condition. Its
main source of revenue is
tourism, yet it retains its dignity
and a sense of life with classy
shops and restaurants. The
church of **Notre-Dame-de-la-
Tronchaye** was built in the 12th
century and was granted
collegiate status in 1498. Its
unusual but harmonious exterior
and 16th-century calvary are
counterbalanced by interior
interest, including a fine gallery
and Renaissance altarpieces.
The **castle** at the top of the town
was restored at the beginning of
this century by two American
brothers who have installed a
small museum.

Medieval washhouses in Vannes

◆◆◆
VANNES

This busy commercial city at the
head of the Golfe du Morbihan
has a long, prestigious history.
Vannes, the capital of the Veneti
(the tribe defeated by Caesar in
56 BC) was the Breton capital
during the Middle Ages, along
with Nantes, until union with
France in 1532. The well-
preserved old quarter lies
behind imposing ramparts, best
observed from the promenade
de la Garenne, a raised walk
beside colourful public
gardens. Vannes's most
picturesque buildings, the old
lavoirs (wash-houses) stand
near the Porte Poterne. The
main sight within the walls is the
Cathédrale St-Pierre, a mixture
of styles from Romanesque to
baroque. Inside the unusual
Rotunda chapel lies the tomb of
Vannes's patron, St Vincent

VANNES

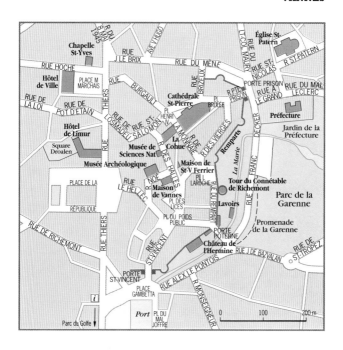

Ferrer, who died in 1419. The house he lived in can be seen in place Valencia. Opposite the cathedral, **La Cohue** is a medieval covered market now used as museum space. A wander through Old Vannes reveals many other handsome buildings and squares, and an eclectic **archaeology museum**. Notice the **Maison de Vannes**, adorned with quaint carvings of a rustic couple popularly known as Vannes and his Wife. The **place des Lices** was once used for medieval tournaments. The canalised **port** reaches as far as the place Gambetta at the southern end of the old town. The **Parc du Golfe**, a leisure park near the *gare maritime*, has several amusements, including a butterfly farm and aquarium.

From Vannes excursion boats ply around the Golfe du Morbihan.

Low-key tourism in historic Vannes

PRACTICALITIES

Accommodation

Arradon
Les Vénètes, La Pointe d'Arradon (tel: 02 97 44 03 11). Peaceful waterside hotel west of Vannes on Golfe du Morbihan. Good views; averagely priced.

Auray
L'Auberge, 56 route de Vannes, Ste-Anne-d'Auray (tel: 02 97 57 61 55). Attractive, old-world inn, traditionally furnished with dark wood and candelabra. Garden. Moderately priced.
La Croix Blanche, 25 rue de Vannes, Ste-Anne-d'Auray (tel: 02 97 57 64 44). Pleasing older-style building on edge of town, decently furnished. Popular haunt with pilgrims. Inexpensive.

Belle-Île
Atlantique, quai de l'Acadie (tel: 02 97 31 80 11). Attractive, well-kept, mid-price hotel by landing stage in Le Palais.
Castel Clara, Anse de Goulphar (tel: 02 97 31 84 21). Luxury hotel-restaurant overlooking picturesque coast. Many facilities (tennis, pool, thalassotherapy).
Phare, Sauzon (tel: 02 97 31 60 36). Simple, pretty building by lighthouse. Excellent value.

Billiers
Domain de Rochevilaine, Pointe de Pen Lan (tel: 02 97 4. 61 61). Unusual village-like complex by sea, luxurious and relaxing, with magnificent views. Expensive rooms and restaurant.

Carnac
La Marine, 4 place de la Chapelle (tel: 02 97 52 07 33).

Well-kept building in town centre, with light clean rooms. Moderately priced.
Les Rochers, 6 boulevard de la Base Nautique (tel: 02 97 52 10 09). Welcoming, mid-priced beach hotel in prime seafront position.

Le Faouët

La Croix d'Or, 9 place Bellanger (tel: 02 97 23 07 33). Handsome building on main square. Averagely priced.

Josselin

Château (tel: 02 97 22 20 11). Imposing dormered building occupying prime site opposite castle. Standard tariff.

Locmariaquer

L'Escale, Dariorigum 2 place (tel: 02 97 57 32 51). Modern waterfront building, plainly furnished but comfortable with good views. Moderately priced.
Lautram, place de l'Église (tel: 02 97 57 31 32). Well-kept small hotel close to harbour. Some garden rooms. Not too expensive. Seafood restaurant.

Ploërmel

Le Cobh, 10 rue des Forges (tel: 02 97 74 00 49). Well-run central hotel. Attractively furnished public areas and well-equipped mid-price bedrooms.

Pontivy

Le Rohan Wesseling, 90 rue Nationale (tel: 02 97 25 02 01). Comfortable business hotel in Napoleonic quarter. Good facilities. Small garden.

Port-Louis

Commerce, 1 place du Marché (tel: 02 97 82 46 05). Practical commercial *Logis* in town centre with restaurant.

Presqu'île de Rhuys (Rhuys peninsula)

Le Mur du Roy, Penvins (tel: 02 97 67 34 08). Low slate-roofed cottage in peaceful coastal location, simply but attractively furnished. Modestly priced. Friendly atmosphere. Restaurant.

Quiberon

Au Vieux Logis, rué des Goëlettes, St-Julien (tel: 02 97 50 12 20). Delightful stone cottage with shutters and flowers and low rates. Restaurant. Garden. Short walk to beach.

La Roche-Bernard

Domaine de Bodeuc (tel: 02 99 90 89 63). Elegant manor in parkland about 3 miles (5km) from town. The intimate, country-house atmosphere. Expensive.
Le Manoir du Rodoir, route de Nantes (tel: 02 99 90 82 68). Fine stone house in English country-house style. Expensive.

St-Nicolas-des-Eaux

Le Vieux Moulin (tel: 02 97 51 81 09). Simple, inexpensive village inn overlooking River Blavet. Comfortable, well-equipped rooms. Restaurant.

Vannes

Le Roof, Presqu'île de Conleau (tel: 02 97 63 47 47). Modern building in peaceful waterfront site some way from old town. Good facilities and spacious, comfortable mid-price rooms. Terraced restaurant.

Eating Out

Arradon

Les Logoden (tel: 02 97 44 03 35). Good-value restaurant in town centre.

La Closerie de Kerdrain, 20 rue Louis-Billet (tel: 02 97 56 61 27). Accomplished, costly traditional fare in attractive Renaissance mansion.

Belle-Île
Contre Quai, rue St-Nicolas, Sauzon (tel: 02 97 31 60 60). Reputable, medium-priced fish restaurant in pretty coastal village.

La Forge, route Port-Goulphar, Le Petit Cosquet (tel: 02 97 31 51 76). Smart, reliable restaurant towards the south of the island. Moderate prices.

Carnac
Auberge de Kérank, route Quiberon, Plouharnel (tel: 02 97 52 35 36). Rustic-style, medium-priced restaurant near Quiberon peninsula.

Le Ratelier, 4 chemin du Douët (tel: 02 97 52 05 04). Country house hotel with good-value food.

Hennebont
Château de Locguénolé, route de Port-Louis, Kervignac (tel: 02 97 76 29 04). Elegant riverside hotel-restaurant. Just about affordable for weekday lunches.

Josselin
Commerce, 9 rue Glatinier (tel: 02 97 22 22 08). Friendly, family-run atmosphere, low prices and splendid castle views.

Lorient
L'Amphitryon, 127 rue Col Müller (tel: 02 97 83 34 04). Elaborate, reverential cuisine for serious foodies. Expensive

Le Victor Hugo, 36 rue Lazare-Carnot (tel: 02 97 64 26 54). Family-run place near marina. Good-value set menus served in spacious, leafy dining room.

Morbihan, Golfe du
L'Escale, Île d'Arz (tel: 02 97 44 32 15). Modern seafront hotel-restaurant. Popular, not too expensive, lunch stopover on gulf cruises. Seafood specialities.

Questembert
Le Bretagne, 13 rue St-Michel (tel: 02 97 26 11 12). Acclaimed Relais de Campagne restaurant with ambitious, expensive nouvelle cuisine in gracious surroundings. Hotel rooms.

Quiberon, Presqu'île de
Ancienne Forge, 20 rue de Verdun, Port-Maria (tel: 02 97 50 18 64). Quiet, pretty place away from seafront. Affordable menu.
La Criée, quai de l'Océan, Port-Maria (tel: 02 97 30 53 09). Informal, inexpensive quayside fish restaurant, popular with families.

La Roche-Bernard
Auberge Bretonne, 2 place Duguesclin (tel: 02 99 90 60 28). Ambitious, expensive food in sophisticated surroundings arranged around garden courtyard. Rooms available.
Auberge des Deux Magots, 1 place du Bouffay (tel: 02 99 90 60 75). Stylish, country-style décor with lively frescoes. Cheerful, unpretentious good-value menus. Rooms available.

Vannes
La Marée Bleue, 8 place de Bir-Hakeim (tel: 02 97 47 24 29). Popular, inexpensive restaurant just outside walls. Copious lunches.
Le Pressoir, 7 rue Hôpital, St-Avé (tel: 02 97 60 87 63). Renowned, high-priced restaurant in rustic-style Louis XIII setting just north of town.

LOIRE-ATLANTIQUE

In 1973 the map of France was redrawn. Brittany's southeastern wing was torn away to form part of a neighbouring region, Pays de la Loire. Many Bretons have never accepted this administrative change, regarding it as another typical Parisian folly. For them the natural boundary of Brittany is still, as it has been for centuries, the final reach of the River Loire. For the purposes of this book, therefore, this *département* is treated as part of Brittany, at least as far as that great southern moat.

As elsewhere in Brittany, the main interest for visitors lies on or near the coast. The beaches are among Brittany's best. Besides the magnificent crescent of sand at La Baule-Escoublac, there are many unspoilt hideaways. Nature lovers will enjoy the fascinating boglands of La Grande Brière, now a regional park, or the strange salt marshes of Guérande. Inland, Loire-Atlantique consists mostly of pleasant but unexceptional farmland. Like the northern borderlands of Haute-Bretagne, however, it boasts several fine castles. Those at Ancenis, Châteaubriant and Grand-Fougeray are notable. Exploring by boat is an interesting option; the waterways around Nantes or the canals of the Grande Brière make good vantage points. Highlight of this *département*, though, is the city of Nantes, Brittany's former capital and one of France's most interesting and lively provincial centres. The old quarter repays at least a day's exploration.

The Nantes-Brest Canal carves through the peaceful Breton countryside

LOIRE-ATLANTIQUE

BATZ-SUR-MER

The low-lying coastline around
Batz is suddenly interrupted by
a tall church spire. This is
St-Guénolé, a 197-foot (60m)
land-and sea-mark above the
salt marshes. Inside it has some
charming features. The chancel
is draped with fishing nets, a
reminder of its seafaring
patronage. The ruined chapel
behind St-Guénolé is **Notre-
Dame-du-Mûrier** (Our Lady of
the Mulberry Tree). Legend
says it was built by a 15th-
century nobleman, saved from
shipwreck by the light of a
miraculous burning tree. In the
village centre is the **Musée des
Marais Salants** (Salt Marsh
Museum), a fascinating
exhibition about the local salt
extracting industry. Batz has
several quiet sandy beaches.
A cliff walk from St-Michel
beach gives good coastal views.

LA BAULE-ESCOUBLAC

La Baule-Escoublac is one of the
smartest and largest resorts in
northern France, vying with the
Riviera for marketable glamour.
At weekends it is packed with
affluent sophisticates from Paris
and other cities. A glorious 3-mile
(5km) beach of gleaming golden
sand is its main attraction,
shelving so gently that you can
safely walk far out to sea within
your depth. Apartment blocks
and large hotels line the seafront
road, some charmlessly modern
and boxlike, others retaining the
style of a more gracious *belle
époque*. La Baule dates back
barely a century. The low-lying
seafront, periodically engulfed in

Loire silt and shifting sands,
supported one precarious fishing
village called Escoublac until
1840, when pine trees were
planted to stabilise the dunes
and provide protection from
winter gales. Gradually a more
favourable microclimate
developed, and in 1879, after the
arrival of the railway, the first
holiday developments began to
appear.

The west side of the resort is the
older and more established
district, with a casino and several
awesomely grand hotels. The
port de plaisance (pleasure boat
harbour) at Le Pouliguen is full of
elegant craft. A channel links the
ocean with the saltmarshes of
Saille. Behind the seafront stretch
tree-lined avenues of seemly
villas dating from the early part
of the century. The **Parc des
Dryades** provides a pleasant
breathing space of neat
municipal gardens and natural
landscaping. From Pornichet, at
the eastern end of the resort,
hydrojet services ply to Belle-Île
and the islands of Morbihan.

La Baule-Escoublac offers every
kind of seaside diversion, from
genteel pursuits like bridge and
golf to the latest high-tech
watersports or thalassotherapy
centres. The streets near **place
de la Victoire** bristle with
appetising shops and restaurants
geared to well-furnished wallets,
and during the season the
resort's social calendar overflows
with multifarious entertainment
and events. La Baule-Escoublac
knows its market, and caters for it
well. If your tastes tend towards
unassuming, inexpensive, or
traditional Breton resorts – La
Baule-Escoublac is not for you.

The port of Le Croisic

◆◆
LE CROISIC

Le Croisic stands at the tip of a peninsula between the Grand Traict lagoon and the sea. Three islets linked by bridges form separate basins in the port, a picturesque scene when the fishing fleets arrive with catches of prawns. A modern *criée* (fish market) occupies one of the islands. Visitors are welcome to watch the proceedings from a gallery, but you will have to get up very early. The pleasantly shabby old town nearby contains 17th-century houses with wrought-iron balconies and dormer windows. **Port-Lin**, on the bracing ocean side of Le Croisic, is the resort, where a cluster of hotels enjoy the waves crashing on dark rocks. Le Croisic's best sight is the splendid **Océanarium**, a modern star-shaped aquarium with well-organised displays of local and exotic species. It is ideal for a wet day but worth a visit in any case. Fish farming exhibits are particularly interesting, and the shark tank has a slightly alarming 'walk-through' tunnel.

◆◆
GUÉRANDE

The medieval ramparts encircling Guérande are visible for miles across the flat surrounding saltmarshes. Inside these tower-studded walls, the old town is a charming assembly of quaint streets with overhanging timber-framed houses. The church of **St-Aubin** has fine capitals and stained glass, and an unusual open-air pulpit. **St-Michel gatehouse** (the former governor's house) contains an idiosyncratic but absorbing museum of local history with displays of

costumes and lifestyles connected with the salt industry. South of Guérande lies a mosaic of glittering pools edged with heaps of salt. Egrets and herons pick their way through the pans in search of fish. Purified salt is sold by the roadside, a useful and inexpensive souvenir (see box below). For more information about this curious landscape, visit the **Maison des Paludiers** (Salt-Workers' House) at Saillé, 2 miles (3km) south. North of Guérande the coastal road reaches the lively sardine-fishing town of **La Turballe**. **Pointe du Castelli** has fine views.

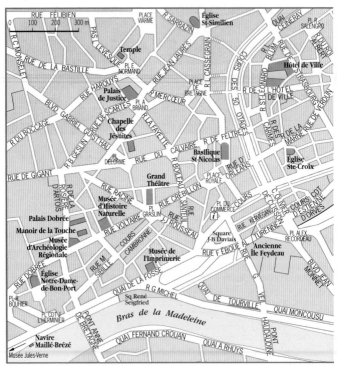

♦♦♦
NANTES ✓

As you approach through a bewildering morass of road systems and industrial suburbs, first impressions of Nantes seem less than enticing. But the central areas are vivacious and full of varied interest, with good shops, restaurants and museums. France's seventh-largest city makes an ideal base for a short break, with the vineyards and châteaux of the Loire Valley close at hand. Boat trips along the Erdre make an enjoyable diversion. Several museums close on Tuesday.

The Gaulish tribe of the Namnetes gave their name to the city, and after the Dark Ages the last Breton king, Alain Barbe-Torte (Crookbeard), chose Nantes as his capital. Anne de Bretagne, Brittany's beloved Duchess, was born in its mighty castle in 1477. In 1598 Henri IV signed the historic Edict of Nantes here, ending religious

NANTES

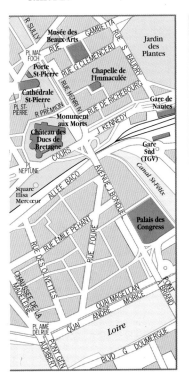

Salt Extraction

The intricate series of pools around Guérande are connected by a network of sluice-gates and drainage channels. Sea water is allowed to flood into the larger lagoons at high tide, trickling gradually into ever-smaller and shallower clay-lined pits to evaporate in the sun and wind. Eventually fine white crystals of table salt (*fleurs de sel*) can be raked from the surface of the water. The greyer, coarser salt beneath is used for cooking or industrial purposes. Each salt pan (*oeillet*) produces about 6,600 pounds (3,000kg) of salt a year. The Breton salt industry dates back to Roman times, and became particularly lucrative in the 16th and 17th centuries, when Brittany enjoyed exemption from the *gabelle* (salt tax). When this privilege was removed during the Revolution, the industry declined.

conflict for almost a century. During the 16th to 18th centuries Nantes lost its political status to Rennes, but prospered economically, partly on the notorious 'ebony' (slave) trade with Africa and the Caribbean. With the silting of the Loire, Nantes became inaccessible to large cargo vessels and diversified into many other industries, though its port activities continue aided by modern dredging techniques. Despite war damage, much of Nantes's attractive 18th- and 19th-century architecture remains intact. Today, Nantes is the thriving regional capital of Pays de la Loire.

The best place to begin exploring is the Castle, or **Château des Ducs de Bretagne**, built by Anne's father François II in 1466. It has altered much in its long history and now houses several museums. The **Musée des Salorges** (Naval Museum) outlines Nantes's part in the slave and sugar trade, and the **Musée d'Art Populaire Régional** (Museum of Local Folk

Nantes's tall cathedral in the upper town

Art) displays clogs, *coiffes* (headdresses) and musical instruments (*open*: daily, except Tuesday, in winter).

Nearby in the upper town is the **Cathédrale St-Pierre**, begun in 1434 and completed over four and a half centuries. Built of bright white tufa, its soaring vaults give an impression of vast space. Highlights include the open-work triforium and the tomb of François II and his wife, the parents of the Duchess Anne. A block or two away, the **Musée des Beaux-Arts** (Fine Arts Museum) contains a wide-ranging collection, strong on 19th- and 20th-century art. The **Jardin des Plantes**, laid out in English style in 1865, contains an extensive collection of ancient magnolias and a huge Palmarium containing a miniature jungle of exotic plants. Towards the lower town, the 15th- and 16th-century houses of **Ste-Croix** and the shipowners' mansions in the **Ancienne Île Feydeau** are full of fascinating detail. Art nouveau and neo-classical buildings stud the grand squares of **place Royale** and **place Graslin**. The **Passage Pommeraye** is a fine 19th-century covered shopping centre. Nantes has over a dozen interesting museums. Beside those already mentioned, the **Palais Dobrée** and the **Musée d'Histoire Naturelle** (Natural History Museum) are particularly interesting. The Palais Dobrée was the former home of a wealthy Nantes shipowner, Thomas Dobrée (1810–95). It contains an excellent archaeological collection and many eclectic objets d'art, including a casket which once held the heart of the Duchess Anne. Among the Natural History Museum's many intriguing exhibits is a drum made from the skin of a soldier (his dying wish).

◆◆
PARC NATUREL RÉGIONAL DE BRIÈRE

A large area north of La Baule Escoublac and St-Nazaire has been designated a Parc Naturel Régional (regional nature reserve). After the Camargue, it is the largest stretch of marshland in France. Before the last Ice Age, this low-lying basin was covered with woodland. When the ice melted and sea levels rose, the area flooded and all the vegetation died, forming a thick layer of peat. Gradually the sea retreated, and eventually the marshes were settled and drained. The native Briérons were granted a ducal charter to exploit the marshes in 1461, and developed an unusual separate way of life based on

hunting, fishing and turf-cutting. Using local reeds to thatch their cottages and make wicker fish-traps, they made their way through the marshes on flat-bottomed punts. Today tourism and the lure of high pay in nearby cities has changed the Brière lifestyle, but with the creation of the park in 1970, the future of the marshes and their rich wildlife is secure. La Grande Brière is now a popular holiday area offering fishing, riding, birdwatching and boating. A circuit of the main villages takes about a day. **Kerhinet** is a cluster of tidily restored cottages (one an *ecomusée*, another an attractive hotel). Several little museums on the Île de Fédrun show how the Briérons once lived, including **La Chaumière Briéronne** (Thatched Cottage), **La Maison de l'Éclusier** (Lock-Keeper's House) and **La Maison de la Mariée** (the Bride's House). The **Parc Animalier** is a nature reserve with walks, hides and information panels (*open*: May to October).

Brière reeds stacked for thatching

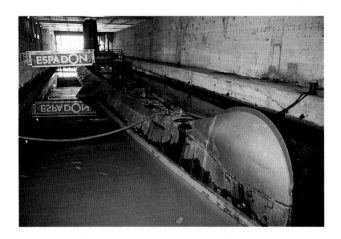

The submarine Espadon *at the Ecomusée de St-Nazaire*

◆
ST-NAZAIRE

Huge deep-water docks and submarine pens made St-Nazaire a target during World War II, though ironically, the concrete pens which once housed German U-boats survived more or less intact. The rest of the city, pounded into rubble by the Allies, was rebuilt after the war in brutal, functional concrete. It now has comparatively few attractions for visitors, though its dockland scene is interesting, and much enhanced by the **Ecomusée de St-Nazaire**, a well-staged display of local history. The best section is the submarine exit, a covered lock containing a French nuclear-powered submarine, *Espadon*, which once sailed the polar ice caps. The shipbuilding industry, once a mainstay of St-Nazaire's economy (several cruise liners were built here) is in sad decline.

PRACTICALITIES

Accommodation

Batz-sur-Mer
Le Lichen, Le Manérick 1¼ miles (2km) southeast on D45 (tel: 02 40 23 91 92). Pleasant seafront hotel with solid, traditional furnishings and average rates.

La Baule-Escoublac
Le Castel Marie-Louise, esplanade Casino (tel: 02 40 11 48 38). Exclusive luxury hotel in *belle époque* mansion with immaculate gardens.
La Palmeraie, 7 allée des Cormorans (tel: 02 40 60 24 41). Attractive, flower-decked villa amid pine trees in quiet location. Reliable, slightly old-fashioned and moderately priced.
Ty-Gwenn, 25 avenue de la Grande Dune (tel: 02 40 60 37 07). Simple, pretty guesthouse with family-run atmosphere offering excellent value. Quiet surroundings, near to beach.

Le Croisic
Les Nids, Plage de Port-Lin (tel: 02 40 23 00 63). Simple but civilised small hotel with partial sea views. Fairly basic and old-fashioned but economically priced rooms.

Guérande
Roc Maria, 1 rue des Halles (tel: 02 40 24 90 51). Old-town gem, all stone and beams. Attractively furnished, with a lovely crêperie.

Nantes
Amiral, 26 bis rue Scribe (tel: 02 40 69 20 21). Neat, practical, modern hotel near place Graslin. Moderate rates.

L'Hôtel, 6 rue Henri IV (tel: 02 40 29 30 31). Chic, suavely designed hotel near castle. No restaurant. Mid-price category.

Le Jules Verne, 3 rue du Couëdic (tel: 02 40 35 74 50). Sleek, black and minimalist, with plenty of plants and gadgetry. Moderate rates.

Eating Out

Batz-sur-Mer
L'Atlantide, 59 boulevard de la Mer (tel: 02 40 23 92 20). Attractive, affordable seafood restaurant along coast road, under same management as Le Lichen (see **accommodation**).

La Baule-Escoublac
Le Castel Marie-Louise, esplanade Lucien Barrière (tel: 02 40 11 48 38). Top-range food in exclusive *Relais et Châteaux* establishment (see also **accommodation**). Book ahead. Elegant, formal, but quite intimate surroundings.

Brière
Auberge du Parc, Île de Fedrun (tel: 02 40 88 53 01). Typical thatched cottage offering good-value local dishes like pike, eel, duck and tench. Special children's menus.

Le Croisic
L'Estacade, 4–5 quai du Lénigo (tel: 02 40 23 03 77). Old-fashioned family-run brasserie, medium-priced menu, popular with locals, near harbour.

Grand Hôtel de l'Océan, Plage de Port-Lin (tel: 02 40 62 90 03). Prime, affordable seafood with Atlantic views. Traditionally smart but comfortable.

Guérande
Les Remparts, boulevard du Nord (tel: 02 40 24 90 13). Good-value menus in traditional hotel by walls.

Nantes
Auberge du Château, 5 place de la Duchesse-Anne (tel: 02 40 74 31 85). Excellent, imaginative food, good value, just opposite castle.

La Cigale, 4 place Graslin (tel: 02 40 69 76 41). Gorgeous *fin-de-siècle* brasserie with intact interior (all panelling, mirrors and mosaic tiles). Good-value seafood lunches and cakes.

L'Esquinade, 7 rue St-Denis (tel: 02 40 48 17 22). Elegant little place near cathedral with cosy, friendly dining room and plenty of choice for a moderate outlay.

Le Mangeoire, 10 rue des Petites-Écuries (tel: 02 40 48 73 83). Excellent country cooking using game, meat and fish. Unpretentious, good-value lunchtime menus.

Peace and Quiet

Wildlife and Countryside in Brittany
by Paul Sterry

Buffeted by westerly gales from the Atlantic, Brittany has some of the most rugged and untamed coastline in France. It is not surprising, therefore, that most visitors to the region are attracted by the stunning scenery and wealth of wildlife found around the shores and spend most of their time within a short distance of the sea. Travel inland for a few miles, however, and you will find heaths, moors and woodland together with a patchwork of small fields and meadows. For anyone interested in peace and quiet, Brittany is indeed an ideal destination.

Les Sept Îles

Lying off the north coast of Brittany, Les Sept Îles are a group of islands that harbour France's most important seabird colonies; it is the only place in France where puffins rear their young. Visitors can land on only one of the islands, Île aux Moines, although boat trips usually provide excellent views

Puffin colonies breed exclusively on the wild headlands of Les Sept Îles

of some of the others; access to Les Sept Îles is by boat from Perros-Guirec between June and August. The ideal time to visit the seabird colonies is in mid- to late June when adult birds will be feeding their young; the sights, sounds and smells of the birds are memorable.

Seabirds

The rich waters that surround the Brittany coast are reflected not only in the seafood served up in local restaurants but also in the numbers of seabirds that favour the region. During the summer months, large numbers of species such as gannets, puffins, razorbills, guillemots, herring gulls and shags fish offshore and nest on some of the more remote or inaccessible cliffs or offshore stacks and islands. In the autumn, the numbers and variety of seabirds increase dramatically as birds from further north in Europe move south on their autumn migration. Birdwatchers should look out for shearwaters, skuas and terns in particular.

PEACE AND QUIET

A female grey seal

Grey Seal

Bobbing at the surface like air-filled bottles, grey seals are often curious about human intruders into their territories. These large, streamlined mammals are fairly common around exposed, rocky coasts in Brittany and are particularly easy to see around the island of Ouessant. Bulls are appreciably larger than cows and are more inclined to drive rival males out of their territory. In the autumn, the cows come ashore to give birth, choosing beaches inaccessible from land or even caves. Although common seals are not thought to breed in the area, they are sometimes seen off the Brittany coast during winter. The species is smaller than the grey seal and has a proportionately smaller, narrower face which can look rather dog-like.

Cap Fréhel

The rocky headland of Cap Fréhel lies on the north coast of Brittany, to the west of St-Malo. A few seabirds breed on the cliffs but more can be seen flying past out to sea. The best times of year for sea-watching are during migration times in April and May, and again in September and October. Strong to gale force northerly winds bring the birds close to land and observers should also look out for grey seals and dolphins. Cap Fréhel is covered by low-growing, wind-pruned vegetation comprising areas of grassland and heathland as well. The latter is at its most colourful in July when the heather is in flower.

Golfe du Morbihan

The best time to visit the Golfe du Morbihan is from September to March. In the autumn, the area is a staging post for large numbers of waders, wildfowl and other wetland and coastal birds with many of these staying for the winter. Ducks such as wigeon and teal are present in good numbers but the area is perhaps best known for its winter population of brent geese. The Golfe du Morbihan is a huge, tidal basin. At low tide, the water drains away to reveal vast areas of mudflats and saltmarshes; these different habitats support the many plant and invertebrate species on which this rich birdlife depends.

Parc Naturel Régional de Brière

This large park lies not far from the coast between the River Loire and the much smaller River

Vilaine. The area comprises a range of wetland habitats with the Grande Brière marsh at its heart; an information centre and the park headquarters are at Île de Fédrun. As well as reed-beds, water-meadows, fens and carr woodland, Brière has an extensive network of canals. These provide one means of getting around the area, in hired boats, but there are also numerous walking tracks. There is birdwatching interest throughout the year although activity is greatest in the spring. The wetland plants are superb in spring and summer and there is always the chance of seeing otter, wild boar or water vole as well.

The spring squill, one of Brittany's unusual plants

Coastal Flowers

Battered by almost constant winds, only the hardiest of plants can survive on the coast; they must also be able to tolerate salt spray and be resistant to desiccation. Those that are successfully adapted, however, often thrive and carpets of thrift, or sea pink, are a familiar sight on many Breton headlands. Most of the plants, the thrift included, flower in spring and visitors should also look out for spring squill, sea campion, scurvy-grass and sea beet. Although low-growing and compact, both features being adaptations to the windy conditions, many of the plants are easily dislodged by trampling. Take care to cause the minimum of damage when visiting an area of coastal flowers.

PEACE AND QUIET

Île d'Ouessant

The small but inhabited island of Ouessant lies off the west coast of Brittany and can be reached by boat from Camaret-sur-Mer; boat trips from Camaret also visit the seabird-covered rock stacks of Tas des Pois. Throughout spring and summer, seabirds can be seen in the waters surrounding the island and a few species nest on Ouessant itself. The location really comes into its own in the autumn, however, when gales can bring large numbers and a great variety of migrant birds here. Seabirds fly by the headlands and tired land birds feed on the open ground or among the gorse and scrub. Species from as far afield as North America and Siberia have been spotted although, not

A purple heron guards its reedbed nest

surprisingly, common European migrants predominate. Ouessant is part of the Armorique Regional Natural Park.

Parc Naturel Régional d'Armorique

This park comprises a mixture of coasts, woodland, heathland and bogs, and also embraces the island of Ouessant (see previous entry); the park headquarters are in Menez-Meur. In parts, the coastal scenery is dramatic and the wind-pruned coastal heathland vegetation is a colourful sight in July when gorse, bell heather and ling are in flower. In the forests, birdlife is most evident in spring. This

Walkers scale the cliff path at Cap Sizun

season is also best for woodland flowers which abound in many places. Interesting mammals found in the area, though rarely seen, include otter, wild boar and fallow deer.

Cap Sizun
Cap Sizun lies some 12½ miles (20km) west of Douarnenez just north of the D7 which itself leads to Pointe du Raz. Here, the Réserve de Goulien protects some spectacular offshore seabird colonies which can easily be viewed from land. Colony activity is greatest between May and July when the birds are feeding hungry and growing young.

Common and scientific names of species	
grey seal	*Halichoerus grypus*
common seal	*Phoca vitulina*
dolphin	*Delphinus delphis*
wigeon	*Anas penelope*
teal	*Anas crecca*
brent goose	*Branta bernicla*
wild boar	*Sus scrofa*
otter	*Lutra lutra*
water vole	*Arvicola terrestris*
thrift	*Armeria maritima*
spring squill	*Scilla verna*
sea campion	*Silene maritima*
scurvy-grass	*Cochleria officinalis*
sea beet	*Beta maritima*
gorse	*Ulex gallii*
bell heather	*Erica cinerea*
ling	*Calluna vulgaris*
puffin	*Fratercula arctica*
gannet	*Morus bassanus*
razorbill	*Alca torda*
guillemot	*Uria aalge*
herring gull	*Larus argentatus*
shag	*Phalacrocorax aristotelis*
shearwater	family *Procellariidae*
skua	family *Stercoraridae*
terns	family *Sternidae*

Practical

This section includes information on food, drink, shopping, accommodation, nightlife, tight budget, special events etc.

FOOD AND DRINK

Brittany is one of France's prime food-producing regions. Over a million Bretons work in agriculture, and over 60 per cent of the land is cultivated. Dairying, stock-rearing, fruit-growing and fish-farming are major concerns, but above all, Brittany is renowned for market vegetables, particularly artichokes, brassicas and potatoes. The range and quality of foodstuffs produced may suggest Brittany is a great gastronomic region. Oddly, though, Breton cuisine is not especially sophisticated compared with other parts of France, and it lacks distinctive local versions of those two great staples – cheese and wine. The white wines produced around Nantes (primarily Muscadet) now belong to the Pays de la Loire, there is still much to enjoy though – particulary seafood and pancakes. Most of Brittany drinks cider, a speciality product of Cornouaille and the Rance valley.

The port of Morlaix. Beyond the viaduct lies the old town

Quality and freshness of ingredients, however, are indisputable, and eating places cater for all tastes and budgets, from humble pancake stalls to revered pinnacles of gastronomy. Breton seafood is predictably superb; the range available in markets and restaurants is staggering. Visit an early-morning *criée* (fish auction), or commercial fish farm for some idea of this marine cornucopia. Mussels, oysters, scallops and crab are prime local products. If you prefer your

The seafood platters are stacked high in Brittany

FOOD AND DRINK/SHOPPING

A café scene in Quimper

fish hot, try a traditional Breton *cotriade*, or fish stew. Freshwater species of fish reach the kitchens too: *brochet au beurre blanc* is a classic dish of pike in the Nantais white butter sauce. Most Breton of all, though, is lobster, often prepared in a special sauce of tomato, shallots and cognac (*homard à l'armoricaine*). On many menus it appears as *homard à l'américaine*, a mis-spelling attributed to a mistake made by a Parisian restaurant. Steak Chateaubriand is the most widely known Breton meat dish. But Brittany is more famous for its dairy produce than its beef. The meat of *pré salé* (salt meadow) lambs raised on the marshes of Ouessant and the Baie du Mont-St-Michel has a delicious salty flavour. *Gigot à la bretonne* (roast leg of lamb with haricot beans) is a local speciality. Hearty peasant soups and casseroles such as *kig-ha-farz* often contain ham or bacon.

Some of France's most succulent chickens come from around Rennes, while the *challan* is a delicious duck from the Nantes region.

Pancakes are Brittany's most famous speciality, a cheap, quick way of satisfying hunger pangs. Once, they were a staple of the Breton diet, replacing bread in poor homes. Two names are used for Breton pancakes: *crêpe* and *galette*. Generally, crêpes are made with a batter of wheat flour and usually have sweet fillings, while the more traditional galettes are made with the heavier buckwheat flour and are often savoury. *Crêpes dentelles* are paper-thin, lacy pancakes, a speciality of Quimper. You will find crêperies everywhere in Brittany, and the variety of fillings offered defies description. Breton desserts tend to be rich and heavy. *Far Breton* is a solid flan usually containing prunes or raisins. *Kouign-amann* is a delicious cake of sugar, butter and almonds, and *galettes de Pont-Aven* (not to be confused with pancakes) are buttery biscuits like shortbread.

SHOPPING

Many of Brittany's most typical souvenirs are edible or potable. Boxes of *galettes*, packets of *crêpes dentelles*, bottles of local cider or the sweet, mead-like *clouchenn* can be found in all tourist resorts. If you have a less sweet tooth, you could stow away a few tins of sardines or Henaff pâté, or jars of fish soup, to bring home. Any Breton town

Local Breton cider on sale

on market day is a feast for the eyes and the camera. A final pre-ferry dash could stock you up with fresh herbs, farmhouse cheeses, *kouign-amann* (almond cake), artichokes or ice-packed shellfish.

If you would like a more permanent reminder of Brittany, traditional crafts can be found in many centres. Particularly good places to look include Landerneau and Quimper, where branches of an appetising shop called **Comptoir des Produits Bretons** sell a wide range of unusual and tasteful wares, including boat woodcarvings and seaweed pictures. Celtic jewellery or carved granite artefacts are also popular. If you have attended any *pardons* or festivals, the sound of an entire community singing hymns, or playing elegiac Breton tunes on traditional instruments like the *bombard* or the *biniou*, will

haunt you for a long time. Look out for recordings on cassette or CD, or even video. In some places you can even buy the instruments themselves. The pottery known as Quimper *faience* is sold widely in Brittany, though prices are quite high for the genuine product, which is hand-painted. Then there are those stripy Breton fishermen's shirts, sweaters and caps. If you have watched any pancake makers at work, you may like to bring back a special pan and the tools of the trade (a *râteau* or rake and a *spatule* – flat knife) to practise perfect Breton crêpes for yourself. If you are keen on antiques, you can find all kinds of things in *brocante* (antique) shops; you may even find yourself the proud possessor of a large piece of traditional Breton oak furniture, a valuable and handsome talking point in any home. Be sure to organise insurance and freight arrangements with a reputable dealer.

ACCOMMODATION

Brittany offers a vast range of accommodation to suit all tastes and pockets. Much of it is self-catering in campsites and *gîtes*. You can also stay in luxurious châteaux, practical hostels, working farms or *chambres d'hôtes* (bed and breakfasts), besides conventional hotels or apartments. The hotels recommended throughout this book have been chosen on the basis of quality, atmosphere and value for money. Small, personal, family-run places in attractive settings have been favoured, and none which gave an unfriendly reception have been included. Book well ahead if you want to stay in popular resorts in July or August. Many hotels close for several months during winter.

Brittany has about 1,000 registered hotels. French **hotels** are officially graded from one to four stars, with an additional 'luxury' category, depending on the level of facilities offered. By law, hotel tariffs must be clearly visible in the reception area and in each bedroom. Prices are usually quoted per room and do not include breakfast. A service charge may be added (in top-range hotels); others may insist on half-board (*demi pension*) in high season. A full list of registered hotels is available from the French Tourist Office. The popular Fédération des Logis de France consortium has over 300 establishments in Brittany, often small, inexpensive, family-run hotels with good home cooking. The Logis directory is available in bookshops.

The term 'bed and breakfast' as understood in Britain or some other countries doesn't quite describe the French **chambres d'hôtes** experience, which is catching on fast. Establishments

A traditional Breton auberge

vary from grand châteaux to simple rural homes. You are generally provided with an evening meal and are expected to join in family life, so it helps if you can speak a little French. Prices may be no cheaper than staying in an hotel, but this is a sociable and interesting way to explore France. Tourist offices can provide information about booking.

A French **gîte** is a self-catering country holiday home, often a converted farmhouse or cottage. To find a good gîte you should book well in advance (the previous autumn if possible). Many belong to a national government-run scheme called Gîtes de France. The French Tourist Office has a list of addresses and phone numbers of private gîtes. Many holiday companies, including Brittany Ferries (one of the largest operators), offer gîtes. Another self-catering option is to stay in purpose-built apartments, known as **résidences de tourisme**. The French Tourist Office publishes a free guide.

Brittany is a great area for camping holidays. For more information, see **Directory – Camping** (page 111).

CULTURE, ENTERTAINMENT AND NIGHTLIFE

Like other Celtic regions, Brittany takes a fierce pride in its cultural identity and heritage. The further west you go, the more pronounced the differences are between Brittany and the rest of France. After centuries of deliberate suppression by French authorities, Breton culture is now keenly fostered in local universities and through the media. For all these efforts, the Breton language is gradually declining. Folk music and dance, however, have experienced a great revival, encouraged by tourism and an increased interest in summer festivals. Try to see one or two of these. The pardon is one of the most distinctive aspects of Breton life. In medieval times it was primarily a religious event, a solemn communal act of contrition. Today it is generally combined with merrier activities involving much feasting and fun. It also provides an opportunity to show off those gorgeous costumes kept in the wardrobe for high days and holidays. The **Special Events** list on pages 104–5 gives some of the most important annual Breton festivals, but be sure to ask the tourist office for a programme of local happenings.

Festivals may continue well into the small hours, but otherwise, Brittany is not a place for nocturnal revelry. Restaurants generally stop serving quite early in quiet places, and then visitors are left to their own devices. Only the major towns and resorts have much in the way of nightlife. St-Malo, Dinard, Quiberon, Bénodet and La Baule-Escoublac have casinos. Rennes, Nantes and Brest entertain their citizens and student populations with a very good range of theatre, concerts and cinema. During the summer months, a few places put on son-et-lumière shows.

WEATHER AND WHEN TO GO

DINARD

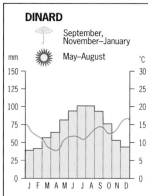

September,
November–January

May–August

Beg-Meil's popular beaches can get crowded in summer

WEATHER AND WHEN TO GO

Brittany's climate is maritime: equable and wettish most of the year. Be prepared for rain at any time. Winter sees few extremes of temperature, and frost and snow are rare. Average daytime temperatures in summer are about 70°F (21°C), a little warmer and drier on the south coast than in the north. Near the sea there is usually a breeze, which may blow up to storm force on the exposed ocean coast.

Brittany's tourist season is short and intense. In July and August beaches, campsites and *gîtes* burst at the seams, but by the end of September the shutters are already falling in a great many resorts. In winter not much happens on the tourist scene. If you have a choice, try to avoid visiting in the peak school holiday season. May/June and September are good times to go, neither crowded nor moribund.

HOW TO BE A LOCAL

Bretons are very used to holidaymakers, and are mostly very welcoming. In a few places, the stresses of a busy tourist season may show by September, with hoteliers and waiters more taciturn than usual. Elementary courtesy should smooth your way. Use your French if you have some. Be ready with *bonjour* and *merci*, at least, and address people as *monsieur*, *madame* and *mademoiselle* in everyday encounters. No one will expect you to speak Breton, but if you show an interest in the language and a respect for local culture you will receive a warm reception.

Bretons are as keen to discuss politics as in any other part of France, but certain topics could arouse heated argument. Brittany's political status is a hot potato in some quarters. It is worth remembering that some Bretons are fervent separatists, and a small minority even ally themselves with the violent tactics of the IRA or the Basque Country's ETA, a trend which is increasingly worrying French authorities. In farming circles, the question of EU import regulations, subsidies, or fishing quotas is a red rag to a bull. In some parts of Brittany, the wartime years are still a vivid and bitter memory.

Brittany is in general a very conservative society, and one of the most intensely religious parts of France. Topless sunbathing may be acceptable on the resort beaches; in town or when sightseeing, dress with decorum. Few places demand formal attire, even for dinner, but leave out the tank tops and sawn-off jeans. Restraint is particularly important when visiting churches and shrines, still a central and revered feature of community life. Festivals are generally jolly affairs when everyone lets their hair down, but a religious *pardon* is a solemn occasion. To be thoroughly welcome (which you are, if properly behaved), blend in with the prevailing mood.

CHILDREN

Brittany specialises in traditional family holidays, and children are welcome almost everywhere.

Seaside refreshments at Dinard

CHILDREN

Accommodation tends to be fairly simple and durably furnished, rather than bursting with priceless antiques and designer fabrics where children (or their parents) may feel ill-at-ease. Restaurants often provide child portions on request, while pancakes are filling, cheap and popular with most children. Reductions on public transport, entrance charges, and child beds are widely available. Many family-oriented hotels or campsites are willing to babysit for an evening while you eat or go out. Beach clubs supervise children in major resorts. Nappies and babyfood can be purchased in all Breton towns, but bring your own supplies if you can. Pushchairs can be difficult to wheel over Brittany's ubiquitous cobblestones!

It is easy to entertain children in Brittany, even if the weather is bad. Lighthouse climbing, castles and boat trips are always popular. Try to catch a fish auction, visit a fish farm, and see a typical Breton festival with costumes and dancing. A short list of some of the best attractions for children follows:

Les Balneïdes, near Beg-Meil. Indoor water park with Brittany's longest water slide.

Château de Hunaudaie. Evocative castle ruins to scramble around.

Château de Josselin. A proper medieval castle, and a marvellous doll collection.

Château de la Bourbansais, near Combourg. Wild animal park and interesting château.

Cobac Parc, Lanhélin. Animals and other amusements.

Domaine de Menez-Meur, Monts d'Arrée. Animal reserve and picnic facilities.

Ecomusée de St-Nazaire. Visit a real submarine.

Ecomusée du Pays de Montfort, Montfort. Charming collection of simple old toys and games.

Ecomusée du Pays de Rennes. Attractive rural life exhibition in an old farm.

Le Galion, Plouharnel. Amazing shell pictures in a replica galleon.

Maison des Minéraux, Presqu'île de Crozon. Geology display with fluorescent rocks.

Moulins de Kérouat, Monts d'Arrée. Restored watermill complex and exhibition.

Musée de la Crêpe, Quimper. All about pancakes, with tastings if you're lucky.

Musée de la Pays Bigouden, Pont-l'Abbé. Good collection of *coiffes* (headdresses) and costumes.

Musée des Télécommunications, Pleumeur-Bodou. Good especially for older children, with lots of hands-on activities (video-telephones, etc) and Radome show. Neighbouring attractions include a Planetarium, and an Asterix-style Gaulish village.

Musée Port-Louis, Port-Louis. Interesting museum complex in a fine fortress. Good for older children, with plenty of ramparts and cannons.

Océanarium, Le Croisic. Splendid, informative aquarium with good ancillary facilities (including ice cream!).

Océanopolis, Brest. Another magnificent aquarium and sea-

centre, Europe's largest. Lots of hands-on activities. Very informative as well as fun.

Parc Naturel Régional de Brière. Lots of things to do, including a barge trip, and several cottage museums.

Port-Musée, Douarnenez. Superbly displayed collection of old boats and maritime buildings. You can go aboard, and watch boats actually being made.

Quic-en-Groigne Galerie, St-Malo. Waxworks provide a painless way of instilling Breton history, in a castle setting.

Zooloisirs, Québriac. Rose gardens, small live animals and extraordinary taxidermy display.

TIGHT BUDGET

● Brittany's holiday season is quite short, with the main surge crammed into July and August. Early or late in the season,

Tasty local produce fills the busy food markets

prices are much lower, though not all facilities are available.

● Inexpensive accommodation options include one- or two-star *Logis* hotels, *chambres d'hôtes*, campsites, *gîtes d'étape*, and *auberges de Jeunesse* (youth hostels).

● Avoid main-square pavement cafés. Ordering and drinking at the bar is always cheaper than waiter service at a table, especially if you sit outside.

● Brasseries, Relais Routiers restaurants, and *ferme auberges* tend to be good value. Choose a simple *prix-fixe* (set-price) menu. Lunchtime set menus, even in quite grand establishments, can be surprisingly cheap, and are a good way to try really accomplished cooking.

● Breton markets are enjoyable and colourful spectacles at any

Breton costumes on parade in Pont l'Abbé

time, but also an excellent place to buy picnic provisions, snacks and souvenirs at much lower prices than shops. Marvellous regional produce is available in Brittany; try local seafood and artichokes.
● Watching pancakes expertly made on a street-stall griddle is a great entertainment; the results are delicious and an astonishingly cheap way of filling sudden internal holes, especially for children. Look out for pancake makers at markets.
● The hypermarkets near the major Channel ports are good places to stock up with wine and French specialities. There are good ones in St-Malo, Roscoff and Morlaix.
● Take film, toiletries, cosmetics and medicaments with you; they may be expensive in resort shops.
● Watch out for special days to visit museums or sights. Sometimes they are free one day a week; on 'Breton Days' many state-run museums are free.
● Good-quality 'seconds' can sometimes be purchased at reduced rates in factory shops, eg the pottery works in Quimper.

SPECIAL EVENTS

Most of Brittany's cultural events and festivals are geared to the short tourist season. Little happens between November and April. Some of the following events are movable feasts and vary from year to year, so if you plan to visit any it is best to check precise dates with the local tourist office.

May
Quintin Pardon
Tréguier Pardon de St Yves

June
Le Faouët Pardon de Ste Barbe
Rumengol Pardon
St-Jean-du-Doigt Pardon du Feu (Pardon of the Fire)

July
Belle-Isle-en-Terre Breton wrestling
Dinan Festival International de la Harpe Celtique (harps)
Fouesnant Fête des Pommiers (apple-tree festival)
Lamballe Festival Folklorique des Ajoncs d'Or (gorse festival)
Locronan Petite (annual) or Grande Troménie (1995 and every sixth year after)
Morlaix Les Mercredis de Morlaix
Nantes Carnival and arts festival
Paimpol Fête des Terre-Neuvas et des Islandais
Pont-l'Abbé Fête des Brodeuses (embroidery festival)
Quimper Festival de Cornouaille
Redon Fête de la Batellerie (canal festival), Festival de l'Abbaye
Rennes Les Tombées de la Nuit
St-Malo Festival de Musique Sacrée
Ste-Anne-d'Auray Grand Pardon
Vannes Grandes Fêtes d'Arvor

August
Cap Sizun Fête des Bruyères (heather)
Carantec Blessing of the Sea
Carnac Grande Fête des Menhirs
Châteauneuf-du-Faou Festival International de Danses et Traditions Populaires
Concarneau Fête des Filets Bleus (blue nets)
Erquy Festival de la Mer
Île de Fédrun Brière Festival
Guingamp Festival de la Danse Bretonne
Lorient Festival Interceltique
Perros-Guirec Fête des Hortensias (hydrangeas)
Plomodiern Fête du Menez-Hom
Pont-Aven Fête des Ajoncs d'Or (gorse flowers)
St-Briac-sur-Mer Fête des Mouettes (seagulls)
Ste-Anne-la-Palud Pardon

September
Camaret-sur-Mer Blessing of the Sea
Le Folgoët Grand Pardon
Fougères Festival du Livre Vivant (historical pageant)
Hennebont Pardon
Josselin Pardon
Penhors Pardon
Trondën Notre-Dame de Trondën Pardon.

SPORT

As one of France's foremost holiday regions, Brittany offers excellent amenities for leisure activities. Most visitors choose coastal destinations, so naturally beach facilities and watersports play an important part in all the seaside resorts. Brittany's changeable climate encourages energetic pursuits rather than passive sunbathing. Today's specialist high-tech sports such as hang-gliding, windsurfing, parascending, scuba-diving and sand yachting are all catered for, as well as more traditional resort pastimes of golf, riding, cycling and tennis. Brittany's network of inland waterways also provides many opportunities to canoe, cruise, sail and fish.

Watersports
There are over 130 Breton sailing schools; Quiberon is one of the best. Sheltered bays, estuaries and inlets, particularly the Golfe du Morbihan and the Rade de Brest, are ideal playgrounds for novices. Elsewhere, treacherous tides, winds, reefs and currents present hazards for the inexperienced. Dozens of regattas and nautical events take place each summer. Windsurfing (planche à voile) and surfing championships take place off the west coast of Finistère, but these waters are strictly for experts. The sheltered south coast and inland lakes like the Lac de Guerlédan are popular for all kinds of watersports.

Windsurfing off the Crozon peninsula

Boating
Canoeing, rowing and kayaking are very popular in Brittany, both on the coast and on inland waterways. Houseboats, narrowboats and cruisers can be hired at many waterway centres, such as Redon. Some are sensibly equipped with bicycles.

Angling
Over 5,600 miles (9,000km) of shoreline and riverbank present a huge range of fishy challenges, from underwater spear fishing to paddling in rockpools for shellfish at low tide. All equipment needed is available locally. No licence is needed for personal consumption, but it is strictly forbidden to sell any fish. Take note of pollution warning signs. Fishing trips can be organised in many ports. Visits to fish farms (eg the mussel *bouchots* of Le Vivier-sur-Mer), make entertaining excursions.

Golf
Brittany has about 30 golf courses, many in lovely coastal settings. Dinard is the oldest and most prestigious course, but etiquette is unstuffy in France. Green fees are around 300F at weekends, but only half as expensive during the week.

Walking
Over 1,500 miles (2,400km) of footpaths cross Brittany, including several GR (*Grandes Randonnées*) long-distance routes with *gîtes d'étapes* (hostels). One (GR380) leads past several famous parish

'Who won that round?' A game of
palet *at Pontivy*

closes and the Monts d'Arrée;
others follow the Emerald and
Pink Granite Coasts. Ask for
walking suggestions at any
tourist office.

Cycling
As in all parts of France, cyclists
are welcomed and catered for.
Cycling events are organised
by each *département*, and bikes
can be hired in any resort. Some
cross-country cycling routes
exist, but footpaths are out of
bounds.

Riding
Organised riding holidays with a
guide or an hour's solitary
hacking are easily arranged at
any of Brittany's *centres*

équestres. Also *roulottes* (horsedrawn caravans) can be hired in
some places.

Breton Games
Like most Celtic regions,
Brittany loves competitive
activities. Trials of strength and
team games play an important
role in community life. Visitors
may see these going on at
summer festivals. Breton
wrestling (*ar gouren*) is rather
like oriental judo, with loose
clothing and ritual kissing.
Other traditional games include
tire-baton, where the
contestants try to lift each other
with a pole, and Breton
versions of hockey and rugby.
You may see locals (usually
men) playing a game called
palet (similar to *boules* but with
discs instead of balls).

Directory

This section contains day-to-day information, including travel, health, documentation, media, money matters and language tips

Contents

Arriving
Entry Formalities

All visitors to France require a valid passport. EU, North American, Japanese, New Zealand and some other nationals require no visa for stays up to three months. Check entry requirements with your nearest French consulate. Several types of visa are available – allow plenty of time to apply (two months is advisable).

By Air

From Paris the choice of Breton destinations is wide: Air Inter, the French domestic airline,

Old houses in Lannion's main square

serves Quimper, Brest, Rennes, Nantes and Lorient. Other airlines serve Dinard, Lannion, Vannes and St-Brieuc. There are also direct flights from the UK, Ireland and the Channel Islands to several airports in Brittany with BritAir (UK tel: 01293 502044; France tel: 02 98 62 77 77), Air France (UK tel: 0181-750 4406; France tel: 02 98 94 30 30), Jersey European Airways (CI tel: 01534 45661), or Aurigny Air Services (CI tel: 01481 822886) – some only in summer.

Some airport cities, such as Nantes and Quimper, are firmly on the European 'weekend break' list. If you are travelling from the US or Canada it is probably best to make your way

DIRECTORY

to Paris and then travel onwards from there; Australasian visitors may find it cheaper to get to Brittany via London.

By Sea
Brittany Ferries (UK tel: 0990 360 360) operate direct sailings to St-Malo and Roscoff from Portsmouth, Plymouth and Poole in the UK (and Cork in Ireland). Services operate all year round. Check brochures carefully for special excursion rates and cheaper sailings. Crossings take between 7½ and 9 hours from Britain (longer from Ireland). From Britain's eastern Channel ports, travellers have a choice of other ferry operators (P&O, Stena Line, Sally Line, Hoverspeed) – and of course the Channel Tunnel. Against apparent gains on shorter crossings you must balance the time and cost of motoring through northern France (including petrol, autoroute tolls, meals and overnight accommodation).

By Train
Fast TGV (*Train à Grande Vitesse*) services enable you to reach Rennes in 2 hours from Paris (Gare Montparnasse); St-Brieuc or Vannes in about 3 hours; and Brest, Lorient or Quimper in 4 hours. Through-fares are available from Britain or Ireland via the Channel ports or Paris (including good-value air/rail deals). By prior arrangement, you can take a bike with you on SNCF, the French state railway (UK tel: 01345 300003 for more information).

By Road
Excellent motorway links (A11 and A81) connect Brittany with Paris and the rest of the French road network. A fast dual carriageway runs via all the major centres around the Breton coast and up through Rennes.

A Brittany Ferry approaches St-Malo

There are no toll roads (*péage*) in Brittany. National Express Eurolines run regular coach services from London via Plymouth/Roscoff to Quimper and Vannes, and via Portsmouth/St-Malo to St-Brieuc (UK tel: 0990 143219). There is also a service to Nantes via Paris.

Camping

Some of France's best campsites can be found in Brittany, especially along the popular holiday coasts of Cornouaille and Trégor. Many are in beautiful settings. Officially they are graded from one to four stars. All are minimally required to have a source of clean running water, daily refuse collection and a telephone. You don't have to use an official site, but *camping sauvage* is strictly prohibited in nature reserves or regional parks. Some sites require you to present a camping *carnet* (permit), available to members of the Automobile Association or from various camping organisations. In July and August many campsites are fully booked, while out of high season facilities may be shut. Any tourist office can supply a list of local campsites.

Car Rental

Except for very short breaks, hiring a car in France is unlikely to be cheaper than bringing your own vehicle across the Channel or from elsewhere in Europe. However, some inclusive holiday packages offer good value and may be worth considering. It is probably cheaper to fix up a car hire deal before you travel, but all the major international car hire firms have desks at airports, ferry terminals and main railway stations. Some companies insist that drivers should be at least 21 years old. If you don't have a credit card you will have to produce a substantial cash deposit when booking. Make sure you sign for collision damage waiver when you take out a contract. You will only need to take out personal accident insurance if it is not covered by your general travel insurance.

Crime

Brittany is generally safe and peaceful but, as in all holiday areas, opportunist theft is a problem. Take out good insurance before you go and don't tempt crime by leaving valuables on view in your car or unsupervised on beaches. Be wary of pickpockets on public transport and in other busy places. If anything is stolen from you, report it immediately to the police, where you will be asked to sign a statement.

Customs Regulations

There is no restriction on duty-paid goods taken from one EU country to another, provided that the goods are carried personally and intended for personal use. Guide limits have been issued stating what is considered suitable for personal use (10 litres of spirits; 90 litres of wine;·110 litres of beer; 800 cigarettes) and if you exceed these you may be questioned closely. Goods bought in duty-

DIRECTORY

free shops (at airports and on ferries) are still subject to restrictions.

Visitors arriving from outside the EU must abide by much tighter regulations when they enter France (currently 200 cigarettes or 50 cigars; 1 litre of spirits or 2 litres of fortified wine or 4 litres of table wine; 60ml perfume and 250ml toilet water).

Disabled Visitors

Facilities for the disabled have improved greatly in France in recent years, though nothing can ease the inconvenience of negotiating Brittany's cobbled streets if you have mobility or visual impairment. A useful publication is *Touristes Quand Même!* which lists facilities for the disabled in many major towns and at tourist sights. Pick up a copy in the UK from the European Bookshop, 5 Warwick Street, London W1R 1RA (tel: 0171-734 5259), or from the publishers, CNFLRH, 38 boulevard Raspail, F-75007, Paris (tel: 01 45 48 90 13). Alternatively, contact Le Comité National Français de Liaison pour la Réadaptation des Handicapés, 38 boulevard Raspail, 75007 Paris (tel: 01 45 48 90 13) or RADAR (Royal Association for Disability and Rehabilitation), 25 Mortimer Street, London W1N 8AB (tel: 0171-637 5400) for advice and information.

Driving

Public transport links the main centres and coastal resorts, but to explore the remoter regions of Brittany at all conveniently, it is best to have a car.

Motor Insurance

Check before you leave your own country that you have comprehensive insurance, and extend your cover if necessary. Many companies offer breakdown cover abroad, including the AA's 5-Star cover, which gives you great peace of mind. It is advisable, though no longer legally required, to carry a Green Card with you, which will provide automatic evidence that you are fully protected if you have an accident. Check your policy with your travel agent if you are booking a package holiday.

Driving Regulations

To drive in France you must be at least 18 years old (possibly older to hire a car), carry a full valid national driving licence (not a provisional licence) and, if you are taking your own car, the vehicle registration document (plus a letter of authorisation from the owner if the car is not registered in your name), insurance documents and a car nationality sticker. Seat belts must be worn by the driver and all passengers, and children under 10 must sit in the back unless in a specially fitted backward-facing seat. Driving is on the right, and headlamp beams must be adjusted on right-hand-drive cars. Carry a red warning triangle in case of breakdown. Drink-driving limits are strict and the police do carry out random breath tests; if you fail, expect a heavy fine or even a driving ban.

Accidents and Breakdowns

If your car breaks down, try to move it off the main highway and flash your hazard warning lights or place a red triangle 33 yards (30m) behind your car. Emergency phones (*postes d'appel d'urgence*) linked to the local police station are placed at 2½-mile (4-km) intervals on main roads and every 1¼ miles (2km) on motorways. If you have an accident, you must call the police (tel: 17 – which also summons an ambulance if necessary). You must also complete and sign an accident statement and exchange insurance details. If possible, try to enlist witnesses at the scene of an accident.

Fines

Hefty on-the-spot fines may be imposed for contravening French traffic regulations. If you

Helpful Euro-signs point the way to the Stone Age

don't carry cash at the time you may be able to proffer vouchers if you have insurance cover. If you consider yourself innocent, you can opt to pay a deposit (*amende forfaitaire*) and the police will issue a receipt.

Priority

Priorité à droite (priority to traffic coming from the right) still causes confusion on French roads, not least among France's own nationals. The rule is still (officially): in built-up areas you must give way to anyone coming out of a side-turning from the right. When approaching roundabouts, give way to any car already on the roundabout. Watch for signs saying *passage protégé*

Parking can be a problem

(meaning you have right of way) or *Vous n'avez pas la priorité* (you don't) and act accordingly. If an oncoming vehicle flashes its lights at you this means its driver has assumed priority.

Roads

There are three types of roads: A stands for *autoroute* (motorway); N is a *route nationale* (main road); D is a secondary road (many roads in Brittany are D roads, even ones that seem quite big). Speed limits are 80mph (130kph) on toll motorways; 68mph (110kph) on dual carriageways and non-toll motorways; 55mph (90kph) on other roads; and 31mph (50kph) in towns (lower in wet or foggy conditions).

Common Road Signs	
chaussée déformée	uneven road surface
gravillons	loose chippings
nids de poules	potholes
déviation	diversion
rappel	watch speed
cédez le passage	give way
absence de marquage	no road markings
ralentir	slow down
route barrée	road closed
passage protégé	right of way
priorité aux piétons	pedestrian right of way
sens unique	one-way street
sens interdit	no entry
toutes directions	route for through traffic

Parking
Don't park where kerbs are marked with yellow paint. Major towns often have *zones bleues* where parking discs must be used (obtain one from the tourist office). Elsewhere there may be meters (2F coins are useful) or complicated signs indicating *Côté du stationnement, jours pairs/impairs* (meaning you can park on one side of the road on alternate days of the month – in other words, odd or even). In towns, multi-storey car parks may be the answer.

Fuel
There are three basic grades of petrol: *gazole* (diesel), *super* (98 octane), and *super sans plomb* (unleaded). The cheapest place to buy petrol is usually at big supermarkets or hypermarkets such as Intermarché.

Route Planning
In high season main coastal routes in Brittany can get very congested. The Automobile Association can tailor-make routes for you or provide advance recorded information on traffic situations in Europe. Maps showing the *Bis* network are available free from roadside kiosks or tourist offices. *Bis* means *Bison Futé* (wily buffalo), a government scheme recommending fast through-routes for holiday traffic.

Road Signs
International European traffic signs are steadily replacing the older ones in Brittany, though you may still find old-fashioned placename signs hewn from granite or set in concrete.

Electricity
Nearly everywhere in Brittany operates at 220 volts, 50Hz. Electric sockets take plugs with two round pins. Take with you an adapter for non-Continental appliances. US and Canadian visitors will also require a voltage transformer for appliances without dual-voltage facility.

Embassies and Consulates
All the main national embassies are in Paris. You should contact them only in dire emergencies, such as the theft of your passport.
Australia 4 rue Jean-Rey, 75724 Paris Cedex 15 (tel: 01 40 59 33 00).
Canada 35 avenue Montaigne, 75008 Paris Cedex 08 (tel: 01 44 43 29 00).
Ireland 12 avenue Foch, 75116 Paris (tel: 01 45 00 20 87).
UK 35 rue du Faubourg-St-Honoré, 75383 Paris (tel: 01 42 66 91 42).
US 2 avenue Gabriel, 75382 Paris Cedex 08 (tel: 01 42 96 12 02).
A consul (or honorary consul) can issue passports, contact relatives and advise on transferring funds. The only ones in Brittany are British and these are at 6 rue Lafayette, 44000 Nantes (tel: 02 40 48 57 47) and at 8 avenue de la Libération, 35800 Dinard (tel: 02 99 46 26 64).

Emergency Telephone Numbers
Police: 17
Fire brigade (*pompiers*): 18
Ambulance (SAMU – *Service d'Aide Medicale d'Urgence*): 15 or 18.

DIRECTORY

Breton oysters can be eaten all year round, but check they're fresh

Health

No vaccinations are specifically required or recommended for travellers to France. Rabies is still technically endemic in France but is very rare in Brittany. To be absolutely safe, don't touch local animals, and if you are bitten seek medical attention however minor the wound. The worst ailment you are likely to suffer in Brittany is an occasional mosquito bite, or (if you are unlucky) a bout of 'holiday tummy', particularly if you enjoy shellfish. Tap water is safe to drink (unless it is labelled *eau non potable*), but bottled water generally tastes better. EU residents are entitled to reciprocal health treatment in France (take the correct form – E111 – with you), but this is no substitute for adequate medical insurance. Check your cover carefully before travelling.

Holidays

New Year's Day – 1 January
Easter Sunday
Easter Monday
Labour Day – 1 May
VE Day – 8 May
Ascension Day
Whitsunday (and Monday)
Bastille Day – 14 July
Assumption Day – 15 August
All Saints' Day – 1 November
Armistice Day – 11 November
Christmas Day – 25 December

Lost Property

If you are unlucky enough to lose something, contact the nearest police station (*gendarmerie* or *commissariat de police*) within 24 hours of discovering the loss. Take your passport (if you still have it!) Obtain a copy of the police report if you intend claiming on your insurance. If you lose your credit cards, contact the nearest bank displaying the appropriate sign (Carte Bleue/Visa or Eurocard/Access).

Media

Foreign newspapers are available in most tourist centres during the tourist season. *Le Monde* and *Le Figaro* are France's biggest national dailies, but the most widely read regional newspaper in France is the Breton *Ouest-France*, which gives details of local events, listings and the other goings-on. *Télérama* lists French radio and television programmes. Besides French national stations such as France Inter (1829m long wave; English-language news bulletins in summer on weekdays at 09.00 and 16.00hrs) or Radio France Bretagne Ouest (93KHz FM; English holiday news at 10.00 and 17.00hrs), the BBC's Radio 4 and World Service can be received in most parts of Brittany. For Voice of America, try FM. Some of the larger hotels are equipped with satellite dishes offering a variety of foreign television channels. France's TV broadcasting system differs from that in the UK. Only black and white portable TV sets will work in France.

Money Matters

French currency is the franc (F or FF), divided into 100 centimes. Notes are issued in denominations of 20, 50, 100, 200 and 500F, and there are coins of 1,2, 5 and 10F, plus 5, 10, 20 and 50 centime pieces. There are no limits on the amount of currency imported, and few visitors need worry about the maximum exportable (50,000F in notes – declare the amount on entry if you are likely to be exporting more).

The safest way to carry large amounts of money is in travellers' cheques (*chèques de voyage*), or Eurocheques if you have a European bank account and the appropriate card. Ask for some small denominations when you order cheques and when you encash them (200F and 500F notes can be difficult to change). Banks with a *Change* sign usually give you the best exchange rate, though many shops and hotels also offer exchange facilities. Banque de France, Banque Nationale de Paris and Crédit Lyonnais generally offer reasonable exchange rates and fairly low commissions.

All major credit and charge cards (*cartes bancaires*) are widely accepted in shops, hotels, restaurants and petrol stations throughout Brittany. Carte Bleue/Visa/Barclaycard is the most popular card in France, although American Express, Diners Club, and Eurocard/ MasterCard/Access are also well known. Check your receipt carefully – no decimal point appears between francs and centimes, but a comma appears instead.

Some retailers are reluctant to accept credit cards for small amounts (below 100F; this should be displayed in the shop). Many banks now have multilingual cash dispensers for customers with credit cards, but you must have a PIN (personal identification number). Alternatively, you can draw cash advances at any bank that displays the Carte Bleue (Visa) or Eurocard (Access) sign.

DIRECTORY

Opening Times

Shops Food shops generally open Monday to Saturday 08.00 or 08.30hrs, while other shops open later (at 09.00 or 09.30hrs). Boulangeries (bakeries) open earlier, and on Sunday too. Half-day closing varies but is often Monday. Lunchtime closing is usually noon to 14.00hrs but supermarkets may stay open all day until late. Nearly every town in Brittany holds a weekly market.

Banks You can generally assume all banks are open at least 09.00hrs to noon and 14.00 to 16.00hrs. Some open Saturday mornings but may close on Monday (beware national holidays – banks close early the day before). Bureaux de change at international airports operate daily 06.00 to 23.00hrs.

Museums and other sights National museums close on Tuesdays, others often on Mondays. Most close on major public holidays. In Brittany, opening hours for tourist sights are very seasonal and summer hours are much longer. Many sights close completely for the winter months (October to Easter). Check opening hours at the local tourist office if there is something you particularly wish to visit. (Ask about admission fees as well, since these vary greatly.) Churches may close at lunchtime, and are sometimes kept locked for security reasons; ask locally who holds the key.

Post Offices These are generally open 08.00 to 17.00, 18.00 or 19.00hrs on weekdays, and 08.00hrs to noon on Saturday. Smaller offices close at lunchtimes.

Pharmacies

Chemists (*pharmacies*) are recognisable by a green cross and are usually open six days a week. Pharmacists in France are

A pharmacy in Nantes

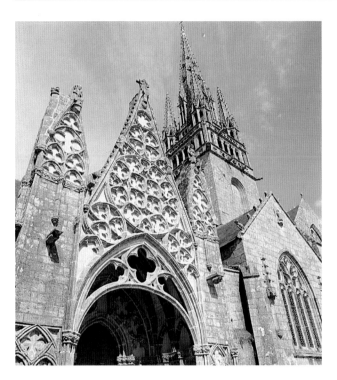

Notre-Dame-du-Roscudon church in Pont-Croix

trained to diagnose and treat minor complaints and can give first aid on request (they may charge a fee). They can also provide the name of a doctor or dentist. They are not allowed to dispense prescriptions from foreign doctors, so take a good supply of any medicines you need regularly. A rota of local pharmacies on duty (*pharmacie de garde*) outside normal hours should be posted on the doors of chemists and in local newspapers, alternatively ask at the police station.

Places of Worship
Brittany is a strongly Catholic region and every town or village has a thriving church community. Check noticeboards to see what time Masses start. Protestant churches can be found in large towns. Other denominations and faiths may be less well represented – ask at the tourist office or town hall.

Police
Police stations are called *commissariats de police* in towns and *gendarmeries* in rural areas (in emergencies, telephone 17). If you lose anything or have a motor accident, report it as soon

as possible and obtain a copy of your statement for insurance purposes. Police in France have the power to levy on-the-spot fines for motoring offences (see **Driving**, page 113).

Post Office

Bureaux de poste can be recognised by the initials PTT or just *Poste*. Correspondence marked *poste restante* may be addressed to any post office in France and collected on proof of identity (passport) for a small fee. You can buy stamps (*timbres de postes*) at tobacconists (*tabacs*) as well as post offices. Post boxes are yellow (free-standing or set into a wall). Use the *départements étrangers* slot for foreign mail. Many post offices have photocopying and fax machines. (See also **Opening Times**, page 118.)

Public Transport

Rail

Brittany has a good network of railways running east–west, connecting all the main centres. North–south travel is rather more complicated. The flagship trains are the high-speed TGVs, for which a premium is charged. There are also *rapide* and express trains, as well as slower local services. Discounts are available for visitors who wish to travel extensively by train. Ask SNCF (the French state railway company) about tourist passes.

Bus

Local buses cover a far wider network of places than the railways and are generally cheaper. They are mostly useful for short hops rather than long hauls. The main bus station in a town is usually found next to the railway station, and some coach services connect usefully with trains. Tickets should be bought on the bus and cancelled (*compostés*) in a machine near the driver.

Boat

Trips to Brittany's islands are highly recommended, as are cruises along its estuaries. Some boats can be chartered on an ad hoc basis for fishing trips or pleasure cruises. Others operate summer excursion programmes depending on demand, including several beautifully restored old craft. You will see trips advertised at harbours, or in local tourist offices. The following companies operate regular summer services:

Emeraude Lines (tel: 02 99 40 48 40) – Rance Valley, Chausey islands, Channel Islands and Fréhel coast from St-Malo and Dinard.

Condor (tel: 02 99 56 42 29) – Channel Islands from St-Malo and Dinard.

Vedettes de Bréhat (tel: 02 96 55 86 99) – Trieux estuary and Île de Bréhat from Erquy, Le Val André, Port Dahouet, Binic, St-Quay-Portrieux and Pointe de l'Arcouest.

Vedettes Blanches (tel: 02 96 23 22 47) – St-Malo to Dinard; Les Sept Îles from Perros-Guirec; bay of Morlaix from Roscoff.

Vedettes Blanche d'Île de Batz (tel: 02 98 61 79 66) – Île de Batz from Roscoff.

Vedettes Armoricaines (tel: 02 98 44 44 04) – Rade de Brest and Presqu'île de Crozon from Brest and Le Fret.

Compagnie Maritime Penn ar Bed (tel: 02 98 80 24 68) – Ouessant and Molène islands from Brest and Le Conquet; Île de Sein from Audierne.

Vedettes Rosmeur (tel: 02 98 27 10 71) – bay of Douarnenez and Presqu'île de Crozon from Morgat and Douarnenez.

Vedettes de l'Odet (tel: 02 98 57 00 58)– Odet estuary from Bénodet, Loctudy, Beg-Meil, Port-la-Forêt, Concarneau and Quimper.

Vedettes Glenn (tel: 02 98 97 10 31)– Odet estuary and Îles de Glénan from Concarneau.

Companie Morbihannaise de Navigation (tel: 02 97 21 03 97) – Belle-Île, Île de Houat and Île d'Hoëdic from Quiberon; Île de Groix from Lorient.

Navix (tel: 02 97 46 60 00) – Golfe du Morbihan from Vannes, Île d'Arz, Île aux Moines, Port-Navalo, Locmariaquer, Le Bono, Auray; Belle-Île from La Trinité-sur-Mer.

Le Côte d'Amour (tel: 02 97 26 31 45) – Golfe du Morbihan from Port-Blanc and Île aux Moines.

Vedettes l'Aiglon (tel: 02 97 57 39 15) – Golfe du Morbihan and Auray estuary from Locmariaquer.

Vedettes Vertes (tel: 02 97 63 79 99)– Golfe du Morbihan from Vannes, Locmariaquer, Port Navalo, Le Bono, Auray and La Trinité-sur-Mer; Auray valley from Vannes.

Vedettes Blanches Armor (tel: 02 97 57 15 27) – Larmor-Baden to Île de Gavrinis (Golfe du Morbihan).

Senior Citizens

Visitors are entitled to reduced or free entrance in many museums and attractions (aged over 60), and fare discounts on public transport (aged over 65). Identification may be required, so it can be worth taking your passport when booking tickets.

Student and Youth Travel

A valid International Student Card or a French *Carte Jeune* may entitle you to substantial discounts on travel, accommodation, admission charges and so on. Enquire about reduced rail or coach fares (Inter-Rail, Eurail) if you are under 26. The Union Française des Centres de Vacances (16 rue de la Santé, 35000 Rennes; tel: 02 99 67 21 02) organises many cultural, leisure and sporting activities for young people. Contact the Association Bretonne des Auberges de Jeunesse (41 rue Victor Schoelcher, 56100 Lorient; tel: 02 97 37 11 65) for information on youth hostels. *Gîtes d'étape* are large country hostels, usually with dormitory-style accommodation, designed for younger people on activity holidays. A booklet called *France Youth Travel* is available from the French Tourist Office (free, but enclose a stamped addressed envelope).

Telephones

Public call boxes in France are generally very efficient and fully operational. In rural areas look for a blue sign saying *téléphone public* on private houses. If you use a phone in a café or restaurant you will probably be surcharged, and if you make a

DIRECTORY

call from a hotel room you will pay a hefty premium.

Telephone numbers in France are usually written and quoted in pairs. They consist simply of ten digits. Cheap rates apply 22.30 to 08.00hrs weekdays, or after 14.00hrs on Saturday at weekends.

You can make international calls from most call boxes but it may be more convenient to use a booth in a post office to save collecting masses of coins. Alternatively, buy a *télécarte* (phone card) in any post office, railway station, *tabac* or newsagent (available in 50 or 120 units, and costing 40F and 96F respectively). To make an international call, lift the receiver, insert the money or card, dial 00, wait for the tone to change, then dial the country code followed by the area code (omitting the initial 0), then the number.

Some international dialling codes are:

  Australia 61
  Canada 1
  Ireland 353
  New Zealand 64
  UK 44
  US 1.

Dial 13 for the operator, 12 for directory enquiries. For reverse-charge (collect) calls ask the operator for a PCV (pronounced: 'pay-say-vay') call (available only to destinations outside France). Calls can be received at phones displaying the blue bell sign.

Time

France is on Central European Time – one hour ahead of GMT for most of the year; six hours ahead of US Eastern Standard Time; nine hours ahead of Pacific Standard Time in California; and nine hours behind Sydney. French summer time begins on the last Sunday in March and ends on the last Sunday in September.

Tipping

Service is usually included in restaurant bills, but a small tip is customary. Porters, taxi drivers, hairdressers and tour guides also expect tips, as at home, though you are under no obligation to reward poor service.

Toilets

Public toilets can be found in shopping centres, petrol stations, hypermarkets and so on. Men are *Messieurs*; women are *Dames* (you may occasionally see the Breton forms *fir* and *mna*). Standards are variable, so take advantage of facilities when you are in cafés, restaurants, hotels or museums, as these are often better kept than average.

Tourist Offices

The French Tourist Office publishes a great deal of literature about France, available from the following addresses:

Australia French Tourist Bureau, BNP Building, 12th Floor, 12 Castlereagh Street, Sydney NSW 2000 (tel: 02 231 5244).

Canada Représentation Française du Tourisme, 1981 Avenue McGill College, Suite 490, Montreal, Quebec H3A 2W9 (tel: 514/1288 4264).

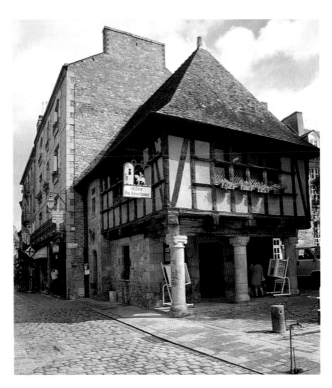

Dinan's quaint Tourist Office

Ireland French Tourist Office, 35 Lower Abbey Street, Dublin 1 (tel: 01-703 4046).

UK French Tourist Office, 178 Piccadilly, London W1V 0AL (tel: 01891 244123).

US French Tourist Office, 610 Fifth Avenue Suite, New York NY 10020-2452 (tel: 212/757 1125). Nearly every small town or resort in Brittany has its own *Office du Tourisme* or *Syndicat d'Initiative* (recognisable by a large letter *i*). Many of these are very seasonal. **Regional tourist office** (Comité Régional de Tourisme) 74B rue de Paris, 35069 Rennes (tel: 02 99 28 44 30).

Côtes-d'Armor Maison du Tourisme, 29 rue des Promenades, BP 4620, 22046 St-Brieuc (tel: 02 96 62 72 00).

Finistère 11 rue Théodore le Hars, BP1419, 29104 Quimper (tel: 02 98 53 09 00).

Île-et-Vilaine 1 rue Martenot, 35000 Rennes (tel: 02 99 02 97 43).

Morbihan Hôtel du Département, rue St-Tropez, BP400, 56009 Vannes (tel: 02 97 54 06 56).

Loire-Atlantique Maison du Tourisme, place du Commerce, 44000 Nantes (tel: 02 40 89 50 77).

LANGUAGE

Despite nationalist dreams and ambitions, the language of Brittany is French. English is spoken widely in Channel port towns (St-Malo and Roscoff) or resorts popular with the English such as Dinard or Bénodet. You don't need to speak a word of Breton to get by in Brittany, but a few words may add to your enjoyment of a visit.

Everyday Breton expressions

good day	demat
goodbye	kenavo
thank you	trugarez
festival	fest-noz
Brittany	Breizh (BZH)
good health	yermat

Breton place names

estuary	aber
river	aven
peak	beg
table	dol
island	enez
church	iliz
castle	kastell
village, house	ker
hermitage	lann
flat stone	lech
mountain	menez
important, big	meur
sea	mor
head, summit	penn
parish	plou
port	pors
rock	roc'h
house	ti

Basic phrases in French

yes	oui
no	non
thank you	merci
please	s'il vous plaît
hello	bonjour

good evening	bon soir
good night	bonne nuit
goodbye	au revoir
can you show me...?	pouvez-vous m'indiquer...?
the way to...?	la direction de...?
where is...?	où se trouve...?
I would like	je voudrais
we would like	on voudrait
how many/ much?	combien?
this one	ceci
that one	cela
that's enough	ça suffit
left	à gauche
right	à droite
near	près
straight on	tout droit
opposite	en face de
what time?	à quelle heure?

Shopping

shops	magasins
food shop	alimentation
baker	boulangerie
butcher	boucherie
delicatessen	charcuterie
fishmongers	poissonnerie
confectioners	confiserie
newsagent	librairie
tobacconist	tabac
chemist	pharmacie
ironmongers	quincaillerie
hairdressers	salon de coiffure

Health

prescription	ordonnance
aspirin	aspirine
stomach pills	comprimés digestifs
sleeping pills	somnifères

A picturesque corner of old town Nantes

INDEX

INDEX

INDEX/ACKNOWLEDGEMENTS

Acknowledgements
The Automobile Association wishes to thank the following photographers, libraries and organisations for their assistance in the preparation of this book.

AA PHOTO LIBRARY 34, 62, 95, 96 (A Baker); 18, 22, 23, 24/5, 27, 28, 31a, 31b, 32, 39, 40, 43, 107, 110, 114, 116, 123 (S L Day); 55 (P Kenward); 101, 106 (B Smith); 6, 10, 12, 13, 14/5, 17, 36/7, 45, 46, 49, 50, 52, 56, 58, 59, 60, 66, 68, 71, 72, 74/5, 79, 81, 84, 85, 86, 93, 94, 97, 98, 100, 104, 108, 118, 119, 125; (R Strange); 4, 11, 16, 48, 69, 76, 103, 113 (R Victor)

EDMUND NÄGELE F.R.P.S F/Cover

NATURE PHOTOGRAPHERS LTD 8/9 (P R Sterry), 88 (P R Sterry), 90 (W S Paton), 91 (P R Sterry), 92 (K Carlson).

Author's Acknowledgement
Lindsay Hunt would like to thank Brittany Ferries and the French Government Tourist Office for their assistance in the preparation of this book.

Contributors for this edition:

Copy editor: Colin Follett   **Verified by:** Lindsay Hunt

Indexer: Marie Lorimer